Observations of White Noise

Observations of White Noise

✦

An 'Acid Test' for the First Amendment

Marc M. Harrold

FOREWORD by Robert M. O'Neil
Director of the Thomas Jefferson Center for the
Protection of Free Expression, Charlottesville,
Virginia

iUniverse, Inc.
New York Lincoln Shanghai

Observations of White Noise
An 'Acid Test' for the First Amendment

Copyright © 2005 by Marc M. Harrold

iUniverse books may be ordered through booksellers or by contacting:

iUniverse
2021 Pine Lake Road, Suite 100
Lincoln, NE 68512
www.iuniverse.com
1-800-Authors (1-800-288-4677)

ISBN-13: 978-0-595-37248-5 (pbk)
ISBN-13: 978-0-595-81645-3 (ebk)
ISBN-10: 0-595-37248-1 (pbk)
ISBN-10: 0-595-81645-2 (ebk)

Printed in the United States of America

To:
My Mother and Father

Contents

Acknowledgements

I would like to acknowledge all of my friends and colleagues at the University of Mississippi School of Law. Special appreciation goes to Poindexter Barnes, Phil Broadhead, Tom Clancy, Dawn Jeter, Don Mason, Celeste Sherwood, and Hans Sinha who make coming to work each day a pleasure.

I would like to specifically mention Tom Arriola, Ace Atkins, G. Beato, Debbie Bell, Vincent Blasi, George Cochran, John Czarnetzky, Sam Davis, Scott Deleve, Kyle Duncan, Amitai Etzioni, Hany Farid, Rick Hardy, John Charles Kunich, Steve Mason, Jack Nowlin, Ryan Phair, Ron Rychlak, Morris Sullivan, Kenneth Starr, Eric Vanatta, and Ron White for their specific contributions to this project and, more generally, for their encouragement and friendship. I also want to thank all of the additional people who took the time to send me pictures, trade e-mails and phone calls, and speak with me about the myriad of issues covered in this book; there are too many to mention by name.

I am extremely grateful to Lauren Webb for her diligent editing, hard work and sharp intellect in helping me complete this project. Special thanks also go to my friend Rachel Pierce, an excellent attorney who helped me with the final draft.

Lastly, I would be remiss if I failed to mention two men that have gone out of their way to help me. Rodney A. Smolla, Dean and Allen Professor of Law at the University of Richmond School of Law has always taken the time to correspond with me about issues and topics related to the First Amendment and I truly appreciate it. Next, I am deeply honored that this book includes a Foreword by Robert O'Neil, Director of the Thomas Jefferson Center for the Protection of Free Expression and Professor of Law at the University of Virginia School of Law. Robert has always been very generous towards me with his time and knowledge and for this I offer my sincere thanks and appreciation. Both of these fine attorneys are noted First Amendment scholars and practitioners with busy schedules; I could not ask for guidance from two more accomplished individuals.

Foreword

The reader of Marc M. Harrold's engaging *Observations of White Noise* might be a lawyer highly learned in the subtleties of First Amendment law, or might equally be a layperson to whom such issues would seem bewildering. The book offers value to both potential readers, and to many in between who may have some background in constitutional law, but have never ventured much beyond the text of the Bill of Rights and perhaps the rudimentary cases.

One of Harrold's central premises is an all-too-often forgotten quality of our uniquely American system of free expression: That we do not require speakers or publishers affirmatively to demonstrate their right to express unpopular views, but rather we presume that such protection exists until and unless the contrary is shown, typically by invoking one of several carefully crafted and narrowly defined exceptions. Those exceptions or qualifications include the obvious–speech that incites imminent lawless action, obscenity, child pornography, "fighting words," defamation of purely private persons, and a very few others. Unless speech fits within one of these exceptions, it is presumptively protected, without need to demonstrate that it serves the core values of the First Amendment. In that profoundly important respect, our approach to speech and press differs from those of many other nations, including some with which we share many values and beliefs.

Starting as he does from that vital premise, however, Harrold wisely wonders whether we have always defined the exceptions in the most logical fashion–and whether our courts may not too casually have conferred protection on some types of speech that really don't deserve such protection. In the process, he poses a series of questions that too seldom get asked, and even less often answered, in the conventional debates about free speech and First Amendment precepts.

Specifically, Harrold asks whether we should not be readier than we are to draw analogies between sexually explicit expression that is properly classified as "obscene" and comparably offensive, or intrusive forms of non-sexual expression. In so doing, he recognizes that he is not the first person to venture what may seem heresy to First Amendment purists, but badly needs attention. He posits that certain forms of violent expression, for example, may be more harmful and less logically acceptable than many sexual images that appeal "predominantly to prurient interest," even though the former enjoy broad constitutional protection while the latter send their creators and purveyors to jail, without considering the relative merits or demerits of either type of message.

Much the same question might well be asked about other material of relatively low social utility that has been brought within the First Amendment, such as "violent pornography" of the sort that Indianapolis and Minneapolis sought to ban until the Federal Court of Appeals for the Seventh Circuit barred such efforts, or the willful desecration of the American flag. Here, however, it should be noted that two of the putatively excluded categories of expressive material–Internet websites that instill fear by encouraging reprisals against abortion providers, and instruction manuals for would-be assassins, have in fact recently been denied First Amendment protection by two federal appeals courts, suggesting that there may be greater flexibility in the system–beyond the specifically defined categories of unprotected speech–than one might suppose as an original matter.

The point is not, however, whether a particular type of expression does or does not come within a specific exception. Courts, lawyers and scholars can and endlessly will differ on that issue, with varying results. Harrold addresses a deeper and more basic question–whether our traditional approach to First Amendment jurisprudence adequately reflects changing conditions and interests in the real world, as the relative rigidity of the exclusionary lines tends to assume. On one hand, it is reassuring that the abiding terms "speech" and "press" have proved flexible enough over the centuries to embrace first radio and television, then cable and fax, and finally the Internet. The subtler question is whether, whatever the *medium,* First Amendment jurisprudence has shown comparable flexibility in adapting to new *messages.* The case that courts have been far less creative when it comes to unfamiliar content surely deserves closer scrutiny.

The area in which Harrold makes perhaps the most compelling case for a second look is that of civil liability for consequences of expressive material. Whether it is a child injured or killed emulating a TV stunt, or a family brutally murdered by a killer acting out the scenario of a book (e.g., *Hit-Man Manual*) or a movie (e.g., *Natural Born Killers*), or the victim of a bizarre accident described in enticing detail by a popular magazine (e.g., *Hustler*), it is the same central issue that Harrold forces us to confront: Whether a civil damage award in a civil suit by one private party against another poses the same threat to free expression and First Amendment values as does a criminal prosecution or an administrative edict–the latter being clearly governmental action to which the First Amendment unambiguously applies.

The courts, by and large, have equated civil damages and government sanctions for First Amendment purposes. Indeed, in the *New York Times* libel case (the fortieth anniversary of which we celebrate this spring), Justice Brennan saw that distinction as unworthy of much attention, so obvious to him and the majority for whom he wrote was the comparability of civil damages and criminal sanctions. Largely because of the certainty of that analysis, the issue has barely been reopened in the ensuing four decades. Yet as Harrold makes clear in the most arresting part of the book, we should not so readily accept even Justice Brennan's *New York Times* judgment as the last word, and in light of changing conditions and interests should periodically reopen the question.

That is precisely what Harrold does, and with a welcome degree of skepticism. He then reviews a host of cases and situations that warrant a second look at the almost casual assimilation of civil and criminal penalties. Yet he wisely stops short of removing civil damage claims from the realm of First Amendment concerns, but instead recognizes a range or spectrum of interests that may locate within a broad range a particular claim with potential impact upon speech or press interests. Indeed, an intriguing series of scales—especially the grid bounded by "ideas" at one end and "overt acts" at the other—admirably illustrate the judgment process that Harrold would find more congenial, and ultimately better integrated with the delineation of values and interests protected by our First Amendment.

This book serves many valuable purposes, and deserves the attention of anyone who is overly comfortable with conventional First Amendment jurisprudence, or believes all that need be said on the subject has been said by the Supreme Court or by traditional scholarship.

Robert O'Neil
Director, Thomas Jefferson Center for the Protection of Free Expression and
Professor of Law, University of Virginia School of Law

Preface

The topics covered in *Observations of White Noise* started out as a number of different law review articles that I later found made better chapters in this work. The book is simply that, my observations about the state of the First Amendment, its scope and design, and its place in popular culture. The First Amendment is truly unique as a legal doctrine with a "charged" undercurrent that defines the boundaries of the very reality we perceive while simultaneously dictating our ability to react and express ourselves within these parameters. Thus, it constantly acts to morph our fluid reality.

This book was more of an evolution than linear creation; more vision than project. It is a compilation of thoughts and ideas collected on used envelopes, an endless array of legal pads, napkins, matchbook covers and whatever else was handy; in no way written from beginning to end with a clear path in mind. As I researched issues I would come across people who had taken significant roles in the cases or acted out to protect their freedoms of speech and expression and I was amazed at their willingness to e-mail me, talk to me, provide quotes or send pictures. The ideas that led to this book were exciting and clear; reducing all of this to a tangible work was muddled and challenging. What you hold in your hands is the result: distilled chaos.

At no time in our history have the freedoms to speak, worship and exchange ideas under our First Amendment been more crucial to the continued success of the democratic experiment that is these United States. The Preamble to the U.S. Constitution expressly acknowledges that our Union would not come easy. It was not to be inevitably linked by shared history, language, nationality or any number of other factors that "unite[d]" many existing nations. The ambitious phrase: "in Order to *form* a more perfect Union, *establish* Justice, *insure* domestic Tranquility…" are telling of this continuing task.[1] There is little doubt that America will continue to diversify. It will progress as a nation of an increasing number of races, nationalities, creeds, religions, preferences, languages ideologies and beliefs. With our differences emerge the inevitable result of majorities and minorities; popular and unpopular opinions, etc. The American experience is an incubator for unpopular, and many times, misunderstood, speech and speech expression. Continued diversification will continue to increase the need for the vital protections of the First Amendment.

In a recent speech, Professor Vincent Blasi stated that "[James Madison] was belated in appreciating the importance of the First Amendment and possibly even its potential meaning."[2] I would suggest that perhaps the greatest need for the First Amendment, and even its core meaning, have not yet been seen or fully understood. But, we must continue to try.

Marc M. Harrold
Oxford, Mississippi
2005

A note on the "Living" Constitution

If the Constitution is meant to be a "living" document, the breath that should be thrust into its lungs should be through the actions of men and women taking an active role in a robust democratic Republic, individuals who must answer for their opinions, actions and votes to a constituency made up *"of the people..."*, limited by a judiciary only by the boundaries granted to them by a static interpretation of the Constitution.[3]

In 1987, Justice Brennan stated, "...the Constitution will endure as a vital charter of human liberty as long as there are those with the courage to defend it, the vision to interpret it, and the fidelity to live by it." Justice Brennan was correct that he was to "defend" the Constitution, as written by the Founding Fathers and methodically amended by the States and *not* the courts. Justice Douglas, dissenting in the landmark 1973 case, *Miller v. California,*[4] expressly addressed the Court's willingness to, in fact, amend the Constitution:

> Those [referring to the Court's earlier obscenity rulings] are the standards we ourselves have written into the Constitution. Yet how under these vague tests can we sustain convictions for the sale of an article prior to the time some court has declared it to be obscene?

...

> Today the Court retreats from the earlier formulations of the constitutional test and undertakes to make new definitions. This effort, like the earlier ones, is earnest and well intentioned. The difficulty is that we do not deal with constitutional terms, since "obscenity" is not mentioned in the Constitution or Bill of Rights...[w]e deal here with a regime of censorship which, if adopted, should be done by constitutional amendment after full debate by the people.[5]

Our Constitutional history speaks clearly of both the opportunity and possibility of legislative amendment rather than rampant judicial expansion and creation to deal with the inadequacies in such a static document. When the U.S.

Supreme Court handed down its shameful decision in *Dred Scott v. Sandford*,[6] was the injustice doused by Justices sensing "penumbras" and conjuring up alchemic-like creations such as "substantive due process?" Clearly not, the cure came from within the Constitution's own inner-genius and sense of resolve: the 14th Amendment.

The Court held:

> [T]hat class of persons only whose ancestors were negroes of the African race, and imported into this country, and sold and held as slaves...[t]he only matter before the court, therefore, is, whether the descendants of such slaves, when they shall be emancipated, or who are born of parents who had become free before their birth, are citizens of a state, in the sense in which the word "citizen" is used in the Constitution of the United States[?]

The Court answered this question:

> [I]t is the judgment of this court, that it appears by the record before us that the plaintiff in error is not a citizen...in the sense in which that word is used in the Constitution;....

There can be little doubt that the clear language of the Fourteenth Amendment was drafted expressly to deal with the injustice of the *Dred Scott* ruling. In direct response the Amendment states, "All persons born or naturalized in the United States, and subject to the jurisdiction thereof, are citizens of the United States and of the State wherein they reside...."

That Amendment to this great "charter" is difficult to come by, and viewed by some as inefficient, is not by accident or by Constitutional folly. It is by design. "Efficiency" in this context translates to five lawyers with life terms standing equal to "the People" and a ratification requiring 2/3 of the States. The proper "vision" needed to "interpret" the Constitution is not expansive, it is introspective and respectful.[7]

It is the irony of many great legal minds, that they did more to compromise the security of the Constitution than any force they perceived would threaten it and necessitate its "defen[se][.]"

1

"Nitty Gritty" the First Amendment

The logical place to begin either a study of, or a discussion about, the First Amendment is the text itself. The First Amendment to the United States Constitution states:

> Congress shall make no law respecting an establishment of religion, or prohibiting the free exercise thereof; or abridging the freedom of speech, or of the press; or the right of the people peaceably to assemble, and to petition the Government for a redress of grievances.

The Unique Character of the First Amendment:

A unique aspect of the First Amendment emerges when its textual conception is compared with the remaining nine Amendments that comprise the Bill of Rights, ratified together in 1791.

Of the ten, the First is the lone Amendment that restricts the actions of Congress expressly instead of conferring protective rights directly to the individual.[8] For example, the First Amendment states that *"Congress shall make no law...,"* whereas the Second Amendment[9] simply states that *"...the right of the people to keep and bear Arms, shall not be infringed"*; the Fourth Amendment states that *"[t]he right of the people to be secure in their persons...shall not be violated..."*; the Fifth Amendment states that *"...nor shall be compelled in any criminal case to be a witness against himself, nor be deprived..."*; the Sixth Amendment states that, *"...the accused shall enjoy the right to a speedy and public trial..."* the Seventh Amendment states that, *"...the right of trial by jury shall be preserved..."*; and the Eighth Amendment states that, *"...nor cruel and unusual punishments inflicted."*

In these other examples, a general right is granted in a positive manner to the "person" or to "the people" or it is stated generally that a right shall not be infringed upon. It seems obvious in these circumstances that the intention was that no part of the federal government (the Bill of Rights was initially a restriction on the federal government; the Fourteenth Amendment "incorporated" the states) could violate these positively-conferred rights. Only the First Amendment is limited only to Congress, a single branch of the federal government, and stated in the negative instead of the positive as are the other nine original Amendments.[10]

If the First Amendment had been written consistently with the general conceptual structure of the remaining Amendments that make up the Bill of Rights it might read something like this:

> The Constitution does not delegate to the United States the right to establish any religion, to be deemed official or otherwise, in any form or manner. The right of the people to exercise a chosen religion; to speak freely; and to peaceably assemble in order to petition the Government for a redress of grievances shall not be infringed upon. The right of the people to establish and maintain a free press shall not be infringed upon.

The use of balancing-tests to construct the boundaries of First Amendment protections also seems inherently improper in light of the clear language of the Amendment. "*Congress shall make no law…abridging the freedom of speech, or of the press…*" If the Founding Fathers had desired a flexible standard with regards to the freedoms of speech, press and assembly, they could have easily chosen words to create a zone of protection more susceptible to the "balancing" of interests the Supreme Court has achieved through its various "tests."

For instance, it is clear that the Fourth Amendment is written with the need for this type of innate "balancing" of interests in mind.[11] The Fourth Amendment states that "people [are] to be secure…,against *unreasonable* searches and seizures,…."[12] The First Amendment's construction could reflect the need for this type of balancing by stating, for instance:

> …; or *unnecessarily* or *unreasonably* abridging the freedom of speech, or of the press; or of the right of the people peaceably to assemble, and to petition the Government for a redress of grievances.

The First Amendment: To Rule by Exceptions:

Coming to understand the current state of First Amendment protections is, in large part, a study of what the Amendment does not protect, what falls outside the "ambit" of First Amendment protection.[13]

1. ***Obscenity:*** Although the two words are sometimes used synonymously, obscenity is not the same as pornography. While both may be offensive to certain individuals, pornography (except child pornography) is protected by the First Amendment whereas obscenity is not.

   Obscenity, at the least, must "depict or describe patently offensive 'hard-core' sexual conduct."[14] Whether a work is obscene will be determined by the application of the three-part test set forth in *Miller v. California*:[15]

   a. whether the 'average person applying contemporary community standards' would find that the work taken as a whole, appeals to the prurient interest;[16]

   b. whether the work depicts or describes, in a patently offensive way, sexual conduct specifically defined by the applicable state law; and

   c. whether the work, taken as a whole, lacks serious literary, artistic, political, or scientific value.[17]

   In (a) & (b), above, it is clear that the Court has carved out an exception to the First Amendment only for speech related to sex. ("…appears to the prurient interest"; and "sexual conduct…")

   The Court has held that the state cannot criminalize the possession of even obscene materials "in the privacy of [an individual's] home."[18]

2. ***Child Pornography:*** Any visual work that depicts children engaging in sexual conduct is child pornography. For a work to be deemed "child pornography" it does not have to be separately obscene, thus, it does not need to satisfy the criteria set forth in the *Miller*-test. The Court, in *New York v. Ferber*,[19] held that the state's interest in preventing the exploitation of children in the creation of child pornography was a "compelling" interest and therefore sufficient to allow total prohibition on child pornography.

   Further, unlike obscenity, the Court has held that due to the "compelling" interest of the state to protect children, even possession of child pornography inside the home can be criminalized.[20]

3. **Fighting Words:** Few Constitutional doctrines have the back-woods quality that the "fighting words" exception to the First Amendment does,...as in *"them's fightin' words...!"*

   Generally, the "fighting words" exception allows the government latitude to criminalize speech that is, "...insulting or 'fighting' words—those which by their very utterance inflict injury or tend to incite an immediate breach of the peace. It has been well observed that such utterances are no essential part of any exposition of ideas, and are of such slight social value as a step to truth that any benefit that may be derived from them is clearly outweighed by the social interest in order and morality."[21]

4. **Incitement:** The regulation of speech that advocates illegal conduct is well-developed within First Amendment jurisprudence. The current test, one that appears to encapsulate the most restrictive aspects of the previous tests is found in *Brandenburg v. Ohio.*[22] *Brandenburg* establishes a two-part test requiring that (1) the advocacy is "directed to inciting or producing imminent lawless action"; and (2) the advocacy is also "likely to incite or produce such action."[23]

5. **True Threats:** In several cases, the Court has created an express exception to the First Amendment for "true threats"[24] and has held that "[t]hreats of violence are outside the First Amendment."[25]

6. **Defamation:** Defamation is an intentional false communication that injures the reputation of another. The communication must be made to a third party. There are two primary types of defamation: slander (oral defamation) and libel (written defamation). Although defamation exists as an exception to the First Amendment, the U.S. Supreme Court has granted limited First Amendment protection to defamatory speech. The Court has held that public figures, including public officials, can only recover damages for a claim of defamation when and if they can prove that the statement was made with "actual malice."[26] The Court has also held that a private figure (non-public figure) that sues a media defendant for defamation may only recover with some showing of fault.[27] If the alleged defamatory statement involves a matter of "public concern," then even a private figure must prove "actual malice" to recover damages.[28]

7. **Commercial Speech:** Similar to defamation, early law did not provide any protection under the First Amendment for "purely commercial advertis-

ing."[29] As such, this type of speech could be regulated generally by the states as a business regulation without specific regards of freedom of speech. The modern test to determine whether a law regulating "commercial speech" violates the First Amendment was set forth in *Central Hudson Gas v. Public Service Commission.*[30]

2

Obscenity: Testing the "Balance" of this "Balancing Test"

Note:

As Bob O'Neil states in the Preface to his fine work *The First Amendment and Civil Liability*, most books have serendipitous origins. While it is true that this entire book had serendipitous beginnings, it is especially true with regards to my thoughts about the requirement that obscenity be limited only to sexual-speech and not expanded to allow individual communities the opportunity to apply a more general standard of "super offensiveness" or repulsiveness.

Several years ago, while talking to a friend about obscenity in some now forgotten context, a commercial featuring an animated stomach came on T.V.[31] The large, pink stomach pumped and gurgled with acid. My friend commented absently that she thought *that* was obscene.[32]

Jump ahead a few years, between the Internet and reality-television it seems we have all become voyeurs. G. Beato, in an article in REASON magazine says it better than I can:

> "Is the difference between eating semen-splattered dog food in a porn movie and eating raw pig rectums on *Fear Factor* really so pronounced that the former deserves a jail sentence while the latter becomes a prime-time major network staple?"

Introduction:

In the landmark 1973 decision, *Miller v. California*,[33] Chief Justice Burger, writing for the majority, referred to the "...somewhat tortured history of the Court's obscenity decisions." Justice Douglas, in a vigorous dissent, chastised the Court for its inability to clearly define "obscenity" and its apparent willingness to incarcerate individuals caught in the confusion:

> Obscenity–which even we cannot define with precision–is a hodge-podge. To send men to jail for violating standards they cannot understand, construe, and apply is a monstrous thing to do in a Nation dedicated to fair trials and due process.[34]

Justice Potter Stewart seemed to openly illustrate the ambiguity in determining what is, and is not, obscene, with the following oft-cited quote:

> I have reached the conclusion, which I think is confirmed at least by negative implication in the Court's decisions since Roth and Alberts, that under the First and Fourteenth Amendments criminal laws in this area are constitutionally limited to hard-core pornography. I shall not today attempt further to define the kinds of material I understand to be embraced within that shorthand description; and perhaps I could never succeed in intelligibly doing so. *But I know it when I see it*, and the motion picture involved in this case is not that.[35]

As we have seen, the history of First Amendment jurisprudence has created the boundaries of the freedom of speech not in the positive, by specifically enumerating what is protected, but in the negative, thus holding that all speech is protected except for pure speech falling into express exceptions, or speech-conduct when the applicable balancing-test is satisfied in favor of the government.

While the creation of a "non-sexual obscenity" doctrine may appear to be a tool for expansive censorship and proscription, a pure approach to examining the protections of the First Amendment requires not only the study the existing exceptions that set the boundaries of expressive protections, but also requires us to analyze the logic and constitutionality of these exceptions themselves. Is the "obscenity-test" found in *Miller v. California*[36] itself "under-inclusive" and content-based?[37] Should the doctrine be expanded to allow "community standards" to be determined outright by a community and allow communities themselves to truly define what is "super-offensive" and thus falls outside of the protections of the First Amendment? Or, should the doctrine be eliminated, and offensiveness, whether sexual or not, whether "super" or not, be treated equally under the standard established under *Cohen*?

The Obscenity Doctrine

In *Miller,* the United States Supreme Court set forth its test for obscenity.[38] The Court expanded the class of express exceptions to the protections of the First Amendment, and held that obscenity, when detected or determined using the *Miller*-test, fell outside of the protections of the First Amendment. *Miller* defines obscenity as a type of super-offensiveness category for speech of a sexual nature and content. Through a determination of its "community standards," a given community can determine (through a jury) that due to its [the speech's] sexual nature, the fact that it lacks "serious literary, artistic, political, or scientific value," and the fact that it is "patently offensive," the speech falls outside of the protections of the First Amendment. With regards to "patent offensive[ness]," it is clear since *Cohen v. California,*[39] that mere "offensive" speech (even patently offensive speech) is protected by the First Amendment. In *Miller,* the Court goes beyond merely offensive speech and allows communities to determine that some sexual-speech is *so* offensive that it reaches the outer-ambit of what the given community will tolerate, and due to the community's finding of this extreme offensiveness, the First Amendment does not apply.

What is not clear is why only speech related to sex can reach this level of super-offensiveness that allows the government to proscribe it differently than super-offensive speech that is related to anything but sex. The U.S. Supreme Court, through the obscenity exception to the First Amendment, has created a content-based constitutional-test that is illogical and inconsistent with the First Amendment itself.

This chapter will examine the development of the "super-offensive" speech-exception category of obscenity and examine how its content-restrictive, sex-only nature has created an illogical, content-based "*Catch-22*"[40] for First Amendment jurisprudence. The Court's wisdom has led it to address content-based speech through the use of a content-based test. Through the sex-only limitation to one of free speech's express exceptions, the Court has left unprotected a particular type of speech that it finds unsavory to a different degree than every other type of speech. In allowing communities the power to "draw a line in the sand" with regards to only a single type of speech, the Court has created a "test" that acts only in accordance with its own puritanical slant. In effect, it appears that the Supreme Court, in an effort to avoid a "national standard" with regards to what amounts to "super-offensiveness," has in reality created its own overall national standard: that communities, and the individuals comprising them, can only be "super-offended" by sexual speech, and thus it is impossible that any non-sexual speech could reach this level of "super-offensiveness."

While at first glance the obscenity exception appears to empower communities to create their own "community standards" and avoid a "restrictive national standard" with regards to sexual-obscenity, the true outcome is that since communities are only free to determine their views and acceptance (or non-acceptance) of sexual speech, every community's standard is initially pigeon-holed by the Court which allows for skewed protections in the overall forum of free speech and expression. By creating the tests, the Court controls the scope of the First Amendment and dictates the outer boundaries of speech by altering the inner boundaries of protection.

I.   *The potential and logical viability of non-sexual obscenity.*

In *American Amusement Machine Association v. Kendrick*,[41] Judge Posner, a noted jurist of the Seventh Circuit Court of Appeals, authored an opinion that goes to the heart of the distinction at issue.[42] This article does not take any issue with this opinion. Posner thoughtfully and methodically analyzed and applied the applicable Supreme Court precedent related to obscenity and the First Amendment. In the opinion, Posner makes a statement that is quite telling to this discussion of the logic and policy behind limiting the obscenity exception only to sexual speech.

> "*In common speech, indeed, 'obscene' is often just a synonym for repulsive, with no sexual overtones at all.*"[43]

Given the fact that the underlying policy for the obscenity doctrine is a type of super-offensiveness (or super-repulsiveness if Judge Posner's understanding of the words' common usage is correct) of a particular community, the logic of limiting obscenity to only sexually-related speech reveals the puritanical bias and slant of the Supreme Court test found in *Miller*. This bias results in a disproportionate lack of protection for sexual-speech, when compared to non-sexual speech, even if in reality both equally offend the community at issue.

Judge Posner correctly identifies that the policies behind the Indianapolis statute at issue:[44] (harm) and the obscenity doctrine (offensiveness) were distinct and thus required different levels of protection under existing First Amendment jurisprudence.[45] This article will discuss whether the obscenity doctrine set forth in

Miller should have a different balance and exist evenly to allow proscription of super-offensive speech regardless of whether or not it is sexual in nature or cease to exist at all as an express exception to general First Amendment protection.

A recent case out of the Western District of Washington (at Seattle) addresses this tension between the legal obscenity defined by the *Miller*-test and a more general obscenity standard governed by reality and logic.

In *Video Software Dealers Assoc. v. Maleng*, the federal district court dealt with the constitutionality of a state law that created penalties for the distribution of certain violent video games to minors.

In holding that the Washington state law violated the First Amendment, the court directly addressed the distinction between legal "obscenity" as determined by the *Miller*-test, and the more general definition of obscenity that could encompass non-sexual materials:

> Defendants correctly point out that the phrase "obscene material" is not inherently limited to sexually-explicit materials. The Latin root "obscaenus" literally means "of filth" and has been defined to include that which is "disgusting to the senses" and "grossly repugnant to the generally accepted notions of what is appropriate."
>
> ...
>
> Graphic depictions of depraved acts of violence, such as the murder, decapitation, and robbery of women in Grand Theft Auto: Vice City, fall well within the more general definition of obscenity. *Nevertheless, the [U.S.] Supreme Court has found that, when used in the context of the First Amendment, the word "obscenity" means only material that deals with sex.*[46]

The question that I will continue to ask throughout this section, in relation to the last sentence above is, "*Why?*" What is the logic, grounded in law or otherwise, in only allowing a community to deem a single type of speech (sexual) outside the boundaries of First Amendment protections when other types of speech are equally as "grossly repugnant" and "super-offensive?"

"Super-Offensive" Non-Sexual Speech
i.   Visual Imagery
i(a)   Movies:

The 1994 movie *Natural Born Killers* set off a chain reaction of violence and bloodshed that reached across the United States and abroad. The film was rated "R" and showed the dramatically violent exploits of Mickey and Mallory, two mass-murderers who gain celebrity status through their crimes. Aside from the most hard-core sadists, there was nothing particularly sexual about the film. Following existing First Amendment jurisprudence, a community, regardless of how offensive they felt the movie was, could not proscribe the movie as obscene or "super-offensive." Similarly, under the existing First Amendment law, no option would be available to them to ban the movie on the grounds that it would be harmful to its viewers, especially its younger viewers. Regardless of how violent the movie and how many strategies to go on a mass-murder spree conveyed, it does not amount to "imminent incitement of violence" and therefore cannot be proscribed under *Brandenburg v. Ohio.*

There is little doubt that if the movie depicted sexual exploits to the same graphic degree that it depicts violence, the movie would be banned as obscene and receive an "X" rating. While not sexual, *Natural Born Killers* would be considered very offensive or obscene (in the common usage of the word) to many Americans. Even Oliver Stone, the director of *Natural Born Killers*, commented on the extreme effect the movie had on its audience stating, "[t]he most pacifistic people in the world said they came out of this movie and wanted to kill somebody."[47] *Natural Born Killers* clearly shows that whether speech is "super-offensive" to a given community's "standards" is actually the second step of the determination of whether a community has control to place the speech outside the protections of the First Amendment because of the taste, tolerance and reaction of the community. The first step has already been completed by the Supreme Court in every instance: that to reach the level of "super-offensiveness" under *Miller*, it must be sexual.

i(b)   Television

In September 1974, NBC aired a film entitled *Born Innocent* to a national audience. The film chronicled the life of an adolescent girl who was living in a state-run home as a ward of the state.

In *Olivia N. v. National Broadcasting Company, Inc.*, the court described one particularly disturbing scene from *Born Innocent*:

> ...the young girl enters the community bathroom of the facility to take a shower. She is then shown taking off her clothes and stepping into the shower, where she bathes for a few moments. Suddenly, the water stops and a look of fear comes across her face. Four adolescent girls are standing across from her in the shower room. One of the girls is carrying a "plumber's helper" waving it suggestively by her side. The four girls violently attack the younger girl, wrestling her to the floor. The young girl is shown naked from the waist up, struggling as the older girls force her legs apart. Then, the television film shows the girl with the plumber's helper making intense thrusting motions with the handle of the plunger until one of the four says, "That's enough." The young girl is left sobbing and naked on the floor.[48]

The court, in *Olivia N.*, expressly states that *Born Innocent* is not constitutionally obscene." The court was correct, under existing precedent, that the "artificial rape" scene in *Born Innocent* is not legally obscene. But, again, given that the policy surrounding the obscenity doctrine is one of offensiveness and not harm, it is not clear logically why a given community's disgust at a scene depicting the shower-rape of an adolescent girl with a "plumber's helper" is not as equally a valid reason to place speech outside the protections of the First Amendment as that which appeals to the "prurient interest."[49]

i(c)   Video Games:

While television, movies and books seem to have inherently expressive qualities, it is the evolution and advancement of video game technology that has cloaked modern video games within the protections of the First Amendment generally. Early video games such as "Pong," "Tempest," and "Space Invaders" did not contain the story lines and advanced graphics of modern video games (*i.e.*, "Grand Theft Auto: Vice City") and did not contain an expressive quality that would likely invoke the protections of the First Amendment. The Eighth Circuit noted: "Whether we believe the advent of violent video games adds anything of value to society is irrelevant; guided by the [F]irst [A]mendment, we are obliged to recognize that 'they are as much entitled to the protection of free speech as the best of literature.'"[50]

In response to the graphic violence in certain modern video games, "disputes have erupted across the country as state and local governments have attempted to regulate the dissemination of violent video games to children. As of this date, (July 5, 2004) no such regulation has passed constitutional muster."[51]

The primary obstacle to these restrictions is the U.S. Supreme Court's insistence that only sexual or "prurient" speech can rise to the level of "super-offensiveness" to allow a community to place it outside the "ambit" of First Amendment protections.

Using an example I have previously cited, the Western District of Washington speaks directly to this issue and the inconsistency between obscenity under the *Miller*-test and a more general, and I argue more logical, definition of obscenity for First Amendment purposes:

> Defendants argue that, even if the video games regulated under the Act are expressive, they fall into one of the few categories of speech that have been historically unprotected, in this case, obscenity. Defendants correctly point out that the phrase "obscene material" is not inherently limited to sexually-explicit materials. The Latin root "obscaenus" literally means "of filth" and has been defined to include that which is "disgusting to the senses" and "grossly repugnant to the generally accepted notions of what is appropriate." *See Miller v. California*, 413 U.S. 15, 18 n. 2, 93 S. Ct. 2607, 37 L. Ed. 2d 419 (1973). Graphic depictions of depraved acts of violence, such as the murder, decapitation, and robbery of women in Grand Theft Auto: Vice City, fall well within the more general definition of obscenity. Nevertheless, the Supreme Court has found that, when used in the context of the First Amendment, the word "obscenity" means material that deals with sex. *Id.* Only "works which depict or describe sexual conduct" are considered obscene and therefore unprotected. State statutes designed to regulate obscene materials must be drafted narrowly to cover only "works which, taken as a whole, appeal to the prurient interest in sex, which portray sexual conduct in a patently offensive way, and which, taken as a whole, do not have serious literary, artistic, political, or scientific value." *Miller*, 413 U.S. at 24, 93 S. Ct. 2607.[52]

The Court's insistence that only sexual content can reach this requisite level of patent, super-offensiveness under *Miller*, is illogical in the overall scheme of community self-determination. In the post-9/11 world, is sex really more offensive than violence? Are *Penthouse* and *Hustler* more offensive than tabloids, *Soldier of Fortune*, and True Detective-type magazines? Are violent video games where players abuse women, steal cars, run from the police, shoot people generally and cops specifically, where blood and gore are the norm really less offensive to certain segments of the society than a video game where players engage in graphic sexual conduct?

A hypothetical illustrates the illogical nature of the *Miller*-test's strict adherence to "sex-only" content. Imagine a video game called *Rave, Rape and Pillage–Sin City 2005* where players roam a virtual city searching for women the game calls "scores." Some of these "scores" are willing; some are not. The player gets the maximum amount of points for being the "complete" HCM (hard-core man) and must torture and grotesquely kill some of the women without raping them, violently rape some of the women leaving them alive, and sense when a "score" is "willing" through various "clues" and have consensual, even romantic (yet always graphic) sex with her.

The visual depictions of the action of torturing and killing the women players do not have sex with (or rape) would be graphically violent and offensive, yet would be protected by the First Amendment. If a player cut off a woman's head and arms with a chainsaw or removed her beating heart, this would be OK and would be protected by the First Amendment. If a player randomly shoots at cops while escaping, no problem, it's just graphic, hard-core violence. When a player moves from torturing a female to having graphic, un-consensual sex with her the game *might* be deemed offensive if it can be shown that this appeals to the prurient interest.

When a player finds a "willing" female, apparently turned on by the machismo of the HCM, the game allows him to have graphic sex with her–both parties enjoy the encounter and are consenting participants. This part of the game, instead of being interactive violence, is interactive sex. Although the two parties are willing, and no violence is involved, this part of the game could clearly be deemed obscene under *Miller*. There is no logical base for the Court's insistence that only sexual speech can rise to this level of "super-offensiveness."

i(d)   The Internet:

Whatever manner in which we, as a society, attempt to "balance" the right of free speech against its potential harms will be tested severely by the Internet. One aspect of the Internet specifically tests even the existing application of the *Miller*-test is the struggle to define "community standards." Given the breadth of the Internet, defining "community standards" relative to the location reached, will perpetuate an inevitable return to the general "national standard" that *Miller* expressly rejected.

Many websites on the Internet may easily reach a level of "super-offensiveness" and, but not for the fact that they do not involve sex, could be proscribed under the obscenity exception to the First Amendment.

A. *The Nuremberg Files:*

In this context, the *"Nuremberg Files"* are materials published on-line, and in some cases, through the use of "Wanted-style posters" to oppose legalized abortion. The tone and tactic of the website is not subtle. The website provides links to "Live Abortion Cams" so viewers can "Watch People Going in and out of Baby Butcher Shops in Your City or Town." The site purports to be collecting information to be used later in criminal, "war-crimes" prosecutions against those who have taken part in legal abortion when "the tide of this nation's opinion turns against the wanton slaughter of God's children..."

In this section, I will discuss whether this type of message, through a website or other published means, could be deemed "obscene" by a given community when applying the proposed non-sexual obscenity doctrine. While the website, and other materials created and distributed by what amounts to the somewhat extreme fringe of the pro-life movement tends to be graphic in nature generally, the main aspect of the materials at issue is the inclusion of personal information about abortion providers. The website published a "virtual scorecard" that included the names (and other information) about doctors previously victimized in some manner. If the doctor was still alive, the name was typed in black. If the doctor had been wounded, the name was "grayed" out. If the doctor had been killed, a line was struck through the name.

In the Ninth Circuit's *en banc* opinion, Judge Pamela Rymer states, "[h]owever offensive or disturbing this might be...being offensive and provocative is protected under the First Amendment." While Judge Rymer is generally correct, due to the inclusion of sexual content, in particular cases a certain level of offensiveness and provocativeness is not protected by the First Amendment: when it is sufficiently sexual and deemed obscene. What remains unclear is why only sexual speech which is highly "offensive or disturbing" can rise to the level of being placed, by the standards of a given community, outside First Amendment protections.

B. *"How-to" Commit Suicide Websites:*

The Church of Euthanasia has one commandment: thou shall not procreate; and four pillars: suicide, abortion, cannibalism and sodomy.[53] The front page of the "church's" website shows a woman's tongue licking one of the World Trade Center towers in a phallic manner as one of the fatal planes crashes into it killing thousands.[54]

The theme of the "church's" website seems to be summed up in the phrase "[s]ave the planet–kill yourself." Are these types of "pro-choice" and sometimes "how-to" commit suicide websites offensive?

At the time of printing it does not appear that any website of this type has been found criminally or civilly liable for the content of these sites. Several instances have been documented linking this type of site to successful suicides. A 21 year-old woman, depressed after the loss of her grandmother, was found hanging by a dog leash in the bathroom doorway. When the body was discovered the website was still on, connected to a website detailing how to hang oneself.[55] A 52 year-old woman rented two helium tanks and committed suicide using the gas. Police found a printout from the Church of Euthanasia's website entitled, "*How to Kill Yourself*," detailing the most efficient way to use helium to end one's life.[56]

Is it unreasonable to believe that a certain community could find this type of website as super-offensive as any sexually-explicit website deemed to be obscene?

C. *Websites containing "Virtual" Child Pornography:*

Child pornography is not protected by the First Amendment. In *New York v. Ferber*, the U.S. Supreme Court distinguished child pornography from other types of sexual speech because of the government's interest in protecting the children exploited during the creation of child pornography.[57] In *Ashcroft v. Free Speech Coalition*, the U.S. Supreme Court considered whether works could be banned that "appear to depict minors but were produced without using any real children."[58] In other words, does the First Amendment protect images that appear to depict child pornography where the state cannot assert its direct interest in protecting children from the inevitable exploitation that is involved in producing "actual" child pornography?

The production of "virtual" child pornography is accomplished in two primary ways. First, there is an expansive market of works depicting adults who are consciously made to look younger.[59] Second, through the use of computer imaging where the images of child pornography are actually created through the use of computer technology. There is some debate as to whether this technology actually exists.

Congress found that:

> "(5) new photographic and computer imaging (sic) technologies make it possible to produce by electronic, mechanical, or other means, visual depictions

of what appear to be children engaging in sexually explicit conduct that are *virtually indistinguishable to the unsuspecting viewer* from unretouched photographic images of actual children engaging in sexually explicit conduct; [and]

(6) computers and computer imaging technology can be used to–

'(A) alter sexually explicit photographs, films, and videos in such a way as to make it *virtually impossible for unsuspecting viewers* to identify individuals, or to determine if the offending material was produced using children;

(B) produce visual depictions of child sexual activity designed to satisfy the preferences of individual child molesters, pedophiles, and pornography collectors; and

(C) alter innocent pictures of children to create visual depictions of those children engaging in sexual conduct;…"[60]

Despite such Congressional findings, some experts in computer-forensics doubt that such technology currently exists. Detective Rick Hardy, a computer forensic examiner with the San Diego Regional Computer Forensics Laboratory, responds:

A current hot topic In the Computer Forensic community is the possibility of the creation of virtual child pornography. The question often asked is, "Is virtual child porn possible." The simple answer is, of course, yes. If you define virtual child pornography as the depiction of children involved in explicit sexual conduct created without the use of actual individuals, a set of stick figures created in Windows Paint could qualify as virtual child pornography. The fact that virtual child porn can be created, though, does not address whether it can be distinguished from actual photographic or movie depictions of real children. The answer, in my opinion, and in the opinion of every expert in the field I have spoken to, is that virtual child porn is, and always will be, distinguishable from the real thing. The reasons are rooted both in technology, and in the history of art.

Real photographic images contain a high content of random information. The human form itself is imbued with random shapes and coloring that give it a lifelike look. To understand why a computer program is incapable of producing an image realistic enough to pass for the real thing, one has to recognize how a computer works. Everything within a computer system is based on mathematical calculations. As such, computers are incapable of producing random information. At best, a programmer needing to emulate randomness in a computer application must rely on a pseudo-random algorithm. If real random output is needed, human intervention is necessary. The routine for creating a truly random PGP key includes typing a series of characters. The interim between keystrokes, which [are] random, and completely out of the control of the typist, is measured by a routine in the program, and stored as random numbers. This allows the key to be created with truly random data. Likewise, to create randomness in an image, human intervention is required. Either a real human being is photographed, and the photo altered (not meeting the definition of "virtual"), or the image is created from the ground up by an artist. The best artists throughout history have had the ability to depict the human form in exacting detail, and yet even the best have fallen short of the standard necessary to create a picture of a human being that anyone would mistake for a photograph. The reasons, as related by those who have studied this phenomenon, have to do with the need to depict the coloring, texture, and lighting of human skin. Creating a single realistic image, such as a painting, requires an incredibly long period of intricate work, which ultimately produces a product that is still distinguishable from the real thing. The software that is available to duplicate this effort in a computer system only provides a different canvas for the same process. The difficulties that exist in other mediums are still present on a computer.

Taking this discussion to the creation of movies, one can point to statistics about the current state of the art provided by Hollywood studios. An example in the public domain would be the 2001 Columbia Pictures' release, "Final Fantasy: The Spirits Within." This picture is generally accepted as the closest thing any studio has produced to a totally virtual movie attempting to emulate real human action. Some quick statistics:

1. The movie consisted of over 140,000 frames (approximately 93 minutes at 25 frames per second)

2. Total cost: $115,000,000.00

3. Time to produce: 4 years

4. 200 Animators, directors, producers, and software engineers

5. The movie used 200 Silicon Graphix Octane Workstations, along with 1,100 custom designed CPUs to create the final product

6. Averaged over the entire project, each second of this film cost more than $20,000.00 to produce

7. The average output of each worker was under 8 seconds of film per year (less than one second per month)

It should be noted further that the human skin depicted in "Final Fantasy" is restricted primarily to the face, neck, arms, and hands, and that sequences where one has a close-up view of these areas constitutes only a small percentage of the film. Also, real human actors were used to obtain the data needed to generate human movements, wearing special body suits that created input for the computer. Anyone having seen how this technique works would understand the difficulty in using it to simulate sexual activity. Having said all this, no one viewing even this final product could mistake it for the real thing.

Based on the above, my answer to the question, "Is virtual child porn that is indistinguishable from the real thing [possible]?" would be an unqualified no.[61]

> Dr. Hany Farid, an expert in computer generated images states:
>
> It is certainly possible to create extremely realistic (clothed) people, young and old. Creating naked people is decidedly harder as it requires more details in the body shape, muscularization, skin tone, hair, and genitals. I believe that the technology does exist to create such images, but that it is difficult and time consuming (from both a technical and artistic point of view). Computer graphics software, however, is becoming increasingly more sophisticated. Coupled with faster and faster computers, I suspect that these types of images will become easier to create over the next three to five years.[62]

Regardless of the debate over whether this technology currently exists, it appears likely that it will become available at some point in the future. A content-neutral obscenity doctrine provides an alternate framework for analysis of virtual child pornography.

In *Ashcroft v. Free Speech Coalition*, the U.S. Supreme Court held that certain provisions of the Child Pornography Prevention Act of 1996 (CPPA) were unconstitutional as the statute proscribed "a significant universe of speech that is neither obscene under *Miller* nor child pornography under *Ferber*."[63]

The Court's ruling in *New York v. Ferber*[64] allowed non-obscene child pornography to be placed outside the protections of the First Amendment "because of the State's interest in protecting the children exploited in the production process."[65] The Court, in *Ashcroft*, considered "virtual" child pornography which was produced without the use or exploitation of any actual child.[66] The Court readily admits that even "virtual" child pornography could be deemed independently "obscene" under *Miller* regardless of the manner in which it had been produced.

The Court generally identifies two primary ways that the CPPA does not "attempt to conform to the *Miller* standard."[67] One of these concerns is directly eliminated by my proposed doctrine of content-neutral obscenity, and the other concern over the breadth of the CPPA is also cured due to the existing viability of the third prong of the existing *Miller*-test.

The *Ashcroft* Court, identifies directly that one of the failings of the CPPA is that "[t]he materials [in question] need not appeal to the prurient interest."[68] The Court is concerned that because of the breadth of the CPPA:

> The materials need not appeal to the prurient interest. Any depiction of sexually explicit activity, no matter how it is presented, is proscribed. The CPPA applies to a picture in a psychology manual, as well as a movie depicting the horrors of sexual abuse. It is not necessary, moreover, that the image be patently offensive. Pictures of what appear to be 17-year-olds engaging in sexually explicit activity do not in every case contravene community standards.[69]

A content-neutral obscenity doctrine would deal effectively with these concerns. First, the fact that the materials need not appeal to the prurient interest is of no concern overall and allows for a more realistic evaluation of the communities actual "standards." Next, the "patently offensive" or hard-core requirements of *Miller* continue to be applicable so such items as a textbook would clearly not be deemed obscene.[70] The last line of the Court's quote is especially telling. The fact that not all pictures of this type "contravene community standards" is the exact reason that the community should not be constrained directly by the "prurient interest" standard when determining what is "super-offensive" to a given community.

With regards to virtual child pornography, it seems counter-intuitive that a community should not be free to place graphic materials depicting "what appears to be" child pornography in the same category with other "super offensive" speech.

D.   The "Calvin Klein" Controversy: "Super-offensive" Content in Commercial Speech

In 1980, nothing came between Brooke Shields (then 15) and her "Calvins." Fifteen years later, the controversial designer released a 60's "picture set"-themed campaign which featured models (some, again, as young as 15) posing in a sleazy suburban "Rec-Room" alongside cheap paneling, paint splashed ladders and gawdy shag carpeting. One ad features a teenage-looking male model being prodded by an off-camera older male voice. The man says such things as: *"You got a real nice look,"* *"How old are you?"* *"Are you strong?"* *"You think you could rip that shirt off of you?"* *"That's a real nice body, you work out?"* *"I can tell."* Another similarly-themed ad features a young girl. A voice tells her that she is pretty as she begins to unbutton her clothes.

Other Calvin Klein ads spawning scrutiny depicted young children holding hands while jumping on a sofa. Two little boys, clad only in CK underwear clasp hands while apparently playing and jumping on the sofa. A similar ad featured two little girls, clad only in CK undergarments, holding hands and jumping on the sofa.

Abercrombie & Fitch is another company that has come under scrutiny for the content and tone of their advertising campaign. A&F's racy 2003 "Christmas Field Guide" publication contained references to group sex and featured a number of young-looking models in suggestive poses bordering on outdoor orgies.[71]

Are these ads obscene? Not under the test set forth in *Miller*. Do they constitute child-pornography? Under the standards the Supreme Court established in *Ferber*, they do not. But could these ads rise to the level of "super-offensiveness" on which *Miller* is premised? It seems that they could. It seems logical that certain communities might be as offended by the indirect sexualization of underage children as much as direct, graphic sex between adults.

E.   The Subordination of Women: Is adult-pornography that acts to objectify women an "idea" or an "injury"?

The Seventh Circuit's 1985 opinion in *American Bookseller Association, Inc. v. Hudnut,* reaches to the heart of why the boundaries of *Miller* are illogical in the overall scheme of First Amendment protections and express exceptions and why the fallacies and gaps in current obscenity law do not provide a logical, balanced or workable standard in the vast arena of ideas and unpopular (perhaps harmful) expression.[72]

The law at issue defined "'pornography' as a practice that discriminates against women."[73] The law defines pornography as "the graphic sexually explicit subordination of women, whether in pictures or in words, that also includes one or more of the following:

1.   Women are presented as sexual objects who enjoy pain or humiliation; or

2.   Woman are presented as sexual objects who experience sexual pleasure in being raped; or

3. Women are presented as sexual objects tied up or cut up or mutilated or bruised or physically hurt, or as dismembered or truncated or fragmented or severed into body parts; or

4. Women are presented as being penetrated by objects or animals; or

5. Women are presented in scenarios of degradation, injury, abasement, torture, shown as filthy or inferior, bleeding, bruised, or hurt in a context that makes these conditions sexual; or

6. Women are presented as sexual objects for domination, conquest, violation, exploitation, possession, or use, or through postures, or positions of servility or submission or display."[74]

Obviously, many of the "works" that would fall under this statute may similarly be judged by a given community to be "obscene" under *Miller*. One example of speech that might be proscribed as pornography in Indianapolis under the law at issue in *Hudnut* that was not found to be obscene under *Miller* was the bathroom-rape scene related to the *Olivia N.* case.

Four older girls "violently attack the younger girl, wrestling her to the floor. The young girl is shown naked from the waist up, struggling as the older girls force her legs apart...." It is not completely clear whether this scene would constitute "graphic" sexually explicit speech as required by the statute, but this type of scene may suffice for section 4, above, in which a woman is "presented as being penetrated by an object," in this case a "plumber's helper."

Is the Indianapolis statute anything more than a community asserting its "community standards" in a legislative, proactive fashion rather than the standard being evaluated in light of judicial precedents and "balancing tests"? It is not completely clear.

It should be noted that the Seventh Circuit was correct in doing what it did in the *Hudnut* opinion: methodically applying Supreme Court precedent as controlling law. The Circuit Court identified the ways in which the Indianapolis statute was insufficient in light of the existing *Miller*-test:

> The Indianapolis statute does not refer to the prurient interest, to offensiveness, or to the standards of the community. It demands attention to particular depictions, not to the work judged as a whole. It is irrelevant under the ordinance whether the work has literary, artistic, political, or scientific value. The City and many amici point to these omissions as virtues. They maintain that pornography influences attitudes, and the statute is a way to alter the socializa-

tion of men and women rather than to vindicate community standards of offensiveness. And as one of the principal drafters of the ordinance has asserted, "if a woman is subjected why should it matter that the work has other value?"[75]

In a "non-sexual" obscenity doctrine analysis, it is the lack of "prurient" interest under *Miller* that is divisive. For instance, if the *Miller*-test was balanced, and content-neutral, (*i.e.* did not require prurient interest as its basis) the separate Indianapolis statute would not be necessary. If a work is not sexual, but is sufficiently "patently offensive" because of its depiction of women, for instance, enjoying rape or being penetrated by "objects or animals," the community could proscribe this work for reaching its definition of "super-offensiveness."

The court categorized the statute as "thought control" because speech that depicts women in a certain way is prohibited whereas "[s]peech that portrays women in positions of equality is lawful, no matter how graphic the sexual content."[76] It is not clear why this is so. General laws against obscenity could be passed in Indianapolis that could deal with graphic sexual content which met the standards in *Miller*, regardless of whether or not it depicted women in a negative manner. The court seems to create an all-or-nothing sense of urgency to justify its ruling, that if it does not strike down the ordinance, "thought control" will soon prevail.

Further, if the "prurient interest" prong of *Miller* was eliminated thus allowing communities to evenly determine what type(s) of speech-content reach a level of "super-offensiveness," the doctrine would continue to judge works as a whole and recognize whether they are, in fact, protected under the First Amendment due to their "literary, artistic, political or scientific value."[77]

ii.   Non-Visual Works:[78]
ii(a).   "Rap" Lyrics:

What *Natural Born Killers* is to the world of offensive movies, certain rap-lyrics are to the world of music. While the lyrics usually have a sexual-overtone, mainstream culture often deems the violent content of the lyrics most objectionable.

The 1997 case in the Southern District of Texas, *Davidson v. Time Warner,*[79] surrounded the controversy accompanying the late Tupac Shakur's *2Pacalypse Now* release. In April, 1992, Ronald Howard sped through Jackson County, Texas in a stolen car. He was pulled over by Texas State Trooper Bill Davidson. (traffic charge unrelated to the theft) Howard, who was listening to a pirated copy of Tupac Shakur's *2Pacalyspe Now* pulled out a 9mm Glock semi-automatic pistol and shot Trooper Davidson to death.

> The lyrics to the song, *Crooked Ass Nigga*, glorify the killing of a police officer:
>
> "I got a nine millimeter Glock pistol…[m]y brain locks, my Glock's like a f-kin' mop,…[t]he more I shot, the more mothaf-ka's dropped…[a]nd even cops got shot when they rolled up."[80]

The lyrics of this song contain nothing even remotely sexual. But, is the song offensive? For many, these lyrics would rise to the level of "super-offensiveness" and, as such, the policy of obscenity would be served if they fit into an express exception to the First Amendment as does sexually-related obscenity under *Miller*. The opinion in *Davidson* reflects a court struggling with the fact that this speech is protected.[81]

> *2Pacalypse Now* is both disgusting and *offensive*. That the album has sold hundreds of thousands of copies is an indication of society's aesthetic and moral decay. However, the First Amendment became part of the Constitution because the Crown sought to suppress the Framers' own rebellious, sometimes violent views. Thus, although the Court cannot recommend *2Pacalpse Now* to anyone, it will not strip Shakur's free speech rights….[82]

In its opinion, the court finds the lyrics "disgusting and offensive."[83] Having called the song both "disgusting and offensive," the court would certainly find the song lyrics to *Crooked Ass Nigga* to be "super-offensive." Yet, Shakur retains full free speech rights in this instance; there exists no express exception that places offensive (even "super-offensive") song lyrics outside of First Amendment protections by a given community due to their offensive nature if they are not otherwise sufficiently sexual.[84]

ii(b).   *Violent Instruction Manuals*

The Hit Man Case:

> "The *Hit Man* case was a breakthrough in modern First Amendment jurisprudence, one that I believe will wear well over time. When seen now through the prism of the terrorist attacks of September 11, the elemental notion that even a society dedicated to freedom of speech need not give shelter to detailed

instruction in murder and violence–published with the intent to aid and abet real killers–seems almost self-evidently sound."[85]

A second example where a given-community may have reasonably found that non-visual works could reach this level of non-sexual "super-offensiveness" was in the "how-to-kill" assassin's manual, *Hit Man: A Technical Manual for Independent Contractors*. This book became the subject of a landmark lawsuit filed on behalf of three victims of a murder-for-hire scheme whose killer followed numerous steps set forth in *Hit Man*. The following statement appears in the opening pages of the book.[86]

> "It is my opinion, that the professional hit man fills a need in society and is, at times, the only alternative to 'personal' justice. Moreover, if my advice and the proven methods in this book are followed, certainly no one will ever know."

On the night of March 3, 1993, James Perry, a Detroit street-thug, and self described minister, brutally murdered Mildred Horn, her eight-year-old quadriplegic son Trevor, and Trevor's nurse Janice Suanders. The two women were shot through the eyes at close range; the boy was strangled. Lawrence Horn, Trevor's father and Mildred's ex-husband, hired Perry to perform the murders. The motive was the $2 million settlement received on behalf of Trevor Horn for the negligence resulting in his permanent paralysis.

In planning and committing the murders, Perry closely followed many of *Hit-Man's* instructions on how to solicit a client and arrange a "hit."

The Fourth Circuit's ruling in *Rice v. Paladin Press* is clearly a landmark decision. The book, *Hit Man*, ends in a somewhat cryptic manner, basically challenging readers to commit murder, not at all in-line with its earlier proclamation that it is for "information purposes only!"[87] The book closes:

> Then, some day, when you've done and seen it all; when there doesn't seem to be any challenge left or any new frontier to conquer, you might just feel cocky enough to write a book about it.

The case spurred a great deal of interest and debate on both sides. Although the settlement between the parties demanded that Paladin destroy the remaining 700 or so copies of *Hit Man*, the text of the book became part of the public domain and was widely available on the internet. One such site indicates that the book was downloaded "~ 2500 times between May 23, 1999 and March 31, 2000." It continues to be available on-line. The *FX* cable-television network produced an original TV movie called *Deliberate Intent* based on the case and Rod Smolla's similarly-titled book.

Should a content-neutral or non-sexually-restrictive obscenity doctrine allow for proscription of a work such as *Hit Man*? Obviously, under the *Miller*-test, the book is not obscene due to the absence of any "prurient interest."

iii.   Non-sexual, but "Obscene" Conduct?

The general test for the constitutional legitimacy of a law proscribing what we could consider "speech-conduct" is found in *O'Brien*, a case stemming from the act of burning a draft card in protest to the Vietnam conflict. Other conduct might be found to be offensive yet legal, under the Court's ruling in *Cohen v. California*, where an individual, again disgruntled over U.S. involvement in Vietnam wore a jacket with "Fuck the Draft" written across the back. Other conduct would not be deemed "expressive" and might be criminalized under a variety of indecency or other types of general statutes.

But, again, if the "obscenity" doctrine is to effectuate even and non-content based boundaries of protection for speech and speech-conduct, it seems that at some point, offensiveness would cross over into the type of "super-offensiveness," albeit non-sexual, that could be placed outside the boundaries of the First Amendment by a particular community in my proposed type of non-sexual obscenity.

Conduct that is not normally present in other types of potentially obscene works or materials, the potential for public speech, or even a "captive audience," presents an important distinction. In *Cohen*, the Court held that individuals should "avert their eyes" to speech and speech-conduct that they did not wish to view. In *Miller*, the Court proscribes a type of expression viewed almost exclusively by those who affirmatively seek it. This is illogical. If "super-offensiveness" is the general policy behind "obscenity," it is not clear why this protection would only be in place for sexual, or prurient speech, especially in situations where the audience could be out in public or are "captive."[88] While the Court may have held that the simple words "Fuck the Draft" on a jacket were merely offensive, and thus, legal, it does not follow that there is not a type of highly offensive, yet non-sexual conduct, that should rise to the level of "super-offensiveness" required by the proposed content-neutral obscenity doctrine.

iii(a).   Flag Burning[89]

In 1984, while the Republican National Convention was being held in Dallas, Texas, Gregory Lee Johnson was outside participating in a protest demonstration that had been dubbed the "Republican War Chest Tour." Johnson's intent was to protest the policies of the Reagan Administration, several Dallas-based corporations and what Johnson would later call "American imperialism." Johnson and others marched through the streets, chanted political slogans, and staged what they called "die-ins" to protest nuclear war. Although it is reported that Johnson took no part in it, some members of the group vandalized buildings with spray-paint and overturned potted plants.

A fellow protester stole an American flag from a flagpole and handed it to Johnson who accepted it. The demonstration halted in front of Dallas City Hall where Johnson unfurled the flag, doused it with kerosene and lit it on fire. As the flag burned Johnson and the other protesters chanted "America the red, white, and blue, we spit on you." In a speech many years later at the University of Southern California, Johnson told students "we came, we saw, we burned...[i]t was a very determined protest. It was meant to be defiant."[90]

Needless to say, several witnesses testified later that they had been "seriously offended by the flag burning."[91] Johnson was arrested, charged with "desecration of a venerated object" and eventually sentenced to a year in prison and fined $2,000.

Otherwise legal conduct, when performed in a certain gratuitous manner, can become offensive. In many cases it has to do with "degree" and the overall circumstances. For instance, even the existing obscenity doctrine set forth under *Miller*, makes a distinction that the pornography in question must be "hard-core" to be deemed obscene.[92]

Are there other types of works or conduct, that when performed in an analogous "hard-core" fashion that could rise to the level of "super-offensiveness" such as the level the *Miller* Court articulated as related to sexually-related materials.

Few acts are as abhorrent to Americans as watching someone burn "Old Glory." Perhaps our distaste and intolerance for this act has increased manifold since the tragic events of September 11, 2001. When limited to its bare substantive conduct, it is not the act of burning a flag generally that outrages and offends a majority of the populace, but rather the actor's disrespect of the flag and the country, by using it as a tool of protest.

In fact, the act of burning a flag, in certain instances, is quite respectful and is the proper way to "retire" a torn or tattered flag. In *Texas v. Johnson*,[93] the Court held that Johnson's conviction under a Texas anti-desecration statute[94] was inconsistent with the First Amendment. Justice Brennan eloquently penned:

> We can imagine no more appropriate response to burning a flag than waving one's own, no better way to counter a flag burner's message than by saluting the flag that burns, no surer means of preserving the dignity even of the flag that burned than by–as one witness here did–according its remains a respectful burial. We do not consecrate the flag by punishing its desecration, for in doing so we dilute the freedoms that this cherished emblem represents.[95]

After applying the *O'Brien* test for speech expression to Texas' desecration law the Court held…"[t]he State's interest in preventing breaches of the peace does not support [Johnson's] conviction because Johnson's conduct did not threaten to disturb the peace."[96] Further the Court held that the "American flag alone" did not justify a "separate juridical category"[97] and therefore Texas' interest in "preserving the flag as a symbol of nationhood and national unity"[98] did not "justify [Johnson's] criminal conviction for engaging in political expression."[99]

It is clear that under the existing framework of speech expression jurisprudence, a state had to assert an interest that would satisfy a facial challenge to a proactive law under *O'Brien*. The requirement to hold that the act of "flag-burning" could sometimes reach the level of "super-offensiveness" to invoke the "non-sexual" obscenity doctrine is not so strict or formalistic yet appears logically, if not yet legally, valid.[100]

iii(b).   Cross Burning

> "*The multiple writings, shifting coalitions, and partial dissents that comprised the opinion were confusing enough to prompt seasoned* NEW YORK TIMES *Supreme Correspondent Linda Greenhouse to observe that* Virginia v. Black *'produced a range of opinions more amenable to a chart than to a verbal description.'*"[101]

(a)   An Example of (non-sexual) Obscene Conduct:

In *Virginia v. Black*,[102] the Court revisited one of our culture's most abhorrent, pathetic and racially-charged forms of expression: cross burning.[103] The Court distinguished the Virginia law at-issue from the anti cross-burning statute it had struck down in *R.A.V. v. St. Paul*,[104] because unlike the statute at issue in *R.A.V.*, "…the Virginia statute does not single out for opprobrium only that speech directed toward 'one of the specified disfavored topics.'"[105]

Given this distinction, the Court held that a state could, consistent with the First Amendment, ban cross burning carried out with the intent to intimidate. Given existing exceptions for "fighting words," [106] and "true threats," [107] it is unsurprising that, assuming it can be shown that the cross-burners intent was to intimidate, a state can criminalize this behavior without offending the First Amendment.[108]

Seemingly, this conduct may not always, but could, reach the level of "super-offensiveness" such that it may be deemed obscene. In *Miller*, the Court expressly sets forth a test that in no way considers the content of with what the speaker (or pornographer) is trying to communicate. Intent is irrelevant. What matters is what "the average person" would perceive about the work. I propose, eliminating the sexual aspects of the *Miller*-test: whether the work "depicts or describes, in a patently offensive way…and whether the work, taken as a whole, lacks serious literary, artistic, political, or scientific value."

It seems that burning a cross where it could be publicly viewed could offend observers to the level of "super-offensive" non-sexual obscenity. That cross burning is a type of "hard-core," albeit non-sexual, communication seems obvious.

Justice Thomas, in dissent, acknowledges the reality that certain symbols (the burning cross) can have in our culture and society:

> A white, conservative, middle-class Protestant, waking up at night to find a burning cross outside his home, will reasonably understand that someone is threatening him. His reaction is likely to be very different than if he were to find, say, a burning circle or square. In the latter case, he may call the fire department. In the former, he will probably call the police.[109]

In the Court's analyses in *R.A.V.* and *Black*, in holding that intent to intimidate an individual generally is consistent with the First Amendment, while restricting the reasoning behind a cross burner's intent to certain factors (*i.e.*, race, color, creed, religion or gender) is constitutionally impermissible. Under a uniform obscenity doctrine based on policies of "super-offensiveness" such factors become irrelevant. Under a uniform doctrine, the reaction of the community rather than the speaker's intent is at issue.[110]

In *Black*, the Court stated that "this sense of anger or hatred [even by the vast majority of citizens] is not sufficient to ban all cross burnings."[111] Why not? Is it unreasonable to think that a group of African-Americans in rural Alabama could be as "offended" by a cross burning as they might be by hard-core pornography? Logically, does "super-offensiveness" towards sexual speech and speech expression justify an express exception to the First Amendment whereas "anger" and "hatred" cannot?

Given the Court's having carved-out an exception to allow communities to self-govern the outer boundaries of their tolerance, it seems illogical and against the spirit of pure First Amendment interpretation to demand that communities only be offended to this degree by that which is sexual, yet not that which is oppressive, hate-driven and historically tyrannical.

(b)   Cross Burning: A Second Analysis:

Can the flames of history illuminate only a single, prohibited message?

In *Virginia v. Black,* the Court expends much energy analyzing the legitimacy of the last section of Virginia's anti cross burning statute which states:

> "Any such burning of a cross shall be prima facie evidence of an intent to intimidate a person or group of persons."[112]

The Court concludes that this is an impermissible "shortcut" due to the variety of factors that may lead to the determination of whether "a particular cross burning is intended to intimidate"[113] and concludes that "[t]he First Amendment does not permit such a shortcut."[114]

The Court correctly acknowledges that not all cross burners choose, or attempt, to convey the same message. "To this day, regardless of whether the message is a political one, or whether the message is also meant to intimidate, the burning of a cross is a symbol of hate."[115]

Justice Souter, who writes concurring in part and dissenting in part, also recognizes that the message intended by the burning of a cross may vary:

> To be sure, that content often includes an essentially intimidating message, that the cross burner will harm the victim, most notably in a physical way, given the historical identification burning crosses with arson, beating, and lynching. But even when the symbolic act is meant to terrify, a burning cross may carry a further, ideological message of white Protestant supremacy. The ideological message not only accompanies many threatening uses of the symbol, but it is also expressed when burning a cross is not meant to threaten but merely to symbolize the supremacist ideology and the solidarity of those who espouse it. As the majority points out, the burning cross can broadcast threat and ideology together, ideology alone, or threat alone....[116]

While Justice Souter and the majority are certainly correct in their assertion that cross burning can "carry" different messages, or attempt to "broadcast" different ideologies, the question remains as to whether these more tenuous messages even fall under the First Amendment due to the overshadowing of the historic message culturally imputed to cross burning.

To analyze flag burning, the Court relied heavily on basic "speech-conduct" analysis set forth under *O'Brien*:

> While we have rejected "the view that an apparently limitless variety of conduct can be labeled 'speech' whenever the person engaging in the conduct intends thereby to express an idea."...we have acknowledged that conduct may be "sufficiently imbued with elements of communication to fall within the scope of the First and Fourteenth Amendments."[117]

In *Virginia v. Black*, the Court basically ignored *O'Brien* and while correctly acknowledging the possibility of differing messages even in conduct that has such clear historical underpinnings, mistakenly gave equal footing to this variety of messages under *O'Brien*.

> In deciding whether particular conduct possesses sufficient communicative elements to bring the First Amendment into play, we have asked whether "[a]n intent to convey a particularized message was present, and [*whether*] *the likelihood was great that the message would be understood by those who viewed it.*"[118]

Although a cross burner may intend different messages, this does not mean that there is a "great" "likelihood that these collateral messages would be understood [by viewers]." As this is the case, it is not clear that the non-intimidating messages even bring the First Amendment "into play" as does the primary message traditionally conveyed by cross burning.

I would conclude that in choosing to publicly burn a cross, the "speaker" is bound by the history of such a pronounced and infamous symbol in our society. Regardless of what the speaker's intention, it is logical that only certain "particularized message(s)" are available to viewers of a burning cross. Since the availability of First Amendment protections for conduct (not "pure" speech or press) is doctrinally tied to both the "intent to convey a particularized message" and the necessity of some level of understanding by those who view the conduct, the First Amendment does not apply to a limitless number of alternate meanings when an individual chooses conduct which, due to history or other factors, will convey a predetermined and static message inherently tied to the given nature of the conduct.[119]

The First Amendment, Obscenity and Privacy
Regulating speech in the "spatial" and "transcendent[al]" zones of privacy

Writing for the majority in a recent decision, Justice Kennedy stated:

> Liberty protects the person from unwarranted government intrusions into a dwelling or other private places. In our tradition, the State is not omnipresent in the home. *And there are other spheres of our lives and existence, outside the home, where the State should not be a dominant presence.* Freedom extends beyond spatial bounds. *Liberty presumes an autonomy of self that includes freedom of thought, belief, expression,* and certain intimate conduct. The instant case involves liberty of the person both in its spatial and more transcendent dimensions.[120]

If we follow Justice Kennedy's lead and analyze the First Amendment with an awareness of how people actually live, we find that the obscenity doctrine has become illogical and untenable. In 1969, the Supreme Court held that "the mere private possession of obscene matter cannot constitutionally be made a crime."[121] In today's society, we do live in various "spheres." (*e.g.*, our homes, our car, time spent online, listening to music, etc.) Is it logical that time spent alone in one's car, or what one possesses to enjoy there, should receive less constitutional protection than the contents of one's home? If a rap recording is banned is mere possession protected in one's house but not in his car?

The reliance on "community standards" in *Miller* has become a tenuous basis for the varying levels of protection under the obscenity doctrine because in reality, where we geographically reside defines us to a lesser degree than it has in the past.

An early internet-obscenity case, *United States v. Thomas*, provided an early indication of the inherent conflict between the community standards doctrine and the Internet. The general distinction emerges when considering the various "spheres" of our modern, technologically assisted existence: public and private.

In sum, even if the *Miller*-obscenity doctrine continues to dictate the boundaries of "public obscenity;" the policing of "private obscenity," or privately-viewed obscenity, is becoming illogical and unnecessary.

In a hypothetical based loosely on the facts in *Thomas*, suppose that a website operator in Whittier, California, sets up an erotic subscription-based website he calls the *"Nastiest Place in America."* A couple in Memphis, Tennessee logs onto the internet and decides to subscribe to the website so they can download pornographic images. None of the images depict children. The "community standards" of Whittier would not deem any of the images to be obscene. The "community standards" of Memphis would deem at least some of the images to be legally obscene. But, who cares?

All of the viewing in this situation is done at a personal computer located inside a private residence. All of the parties are consenting adults. In situations where some type of public or underage viewing was occurring, valid time, place, and manner restrictions would suffice. *Stanley v. Georgia* provides that if all of the images were in "hard copy" form (regardless of whether they are legally obscene in the community they are present) those in possession could not be prosecuted. It appears that the only time the electronic data is criminalized when it is "in transit" and thus un-viewable. Attempting to apply the "community standards" doctrine to the internet is illogical and, effectively, recreates the national standard that *Miller* attempted to avoid.[122]

The Continued Viability of Miller's Third Prong

In the following section, I detail the importance of the third-prong of *Miller*, and its continued viability in my proposed doctrine of non-sexual obscenity. In discussing the third-prong, I can't pass on the chance to share part of Utah Chief Justice Ellett's opinion in the 1977 case *Salt Lake City v. Piepenburg* where he candidly comments on his opinion of *Miller's* third-prong and the Justices and Judges who apply it:

> "The motion picture exhibited revealed an entirely naked man and woman in various acts of sodomy (fellatio, cunnilingus, buggery) [it seems there was something else there besides a man and woman] and adultery all shown with closeup camera photography.

> A more sickening, disgusting, depraved showing cannot be imagined. However, certain justices of the Supreme Court of the United States have said that before a matter can be held to be obscene, it must be '…when taken as a whole, lacks serious literary, artistic, political or scientific value.'

> Some state judges, acting the part of sycophants, echo that doctrine. It would appear that such an argument ought only to be advanced by depraved, men-

tally deficient, mind-warped queers. Judges who seek to find technical excuses to permit such pictures to be shown under the pretense of finding some intrinsic value to it are reminiscent of a dog that returns to his vomit in search of some morsel in the filth which may have some redeeming value to his own taste. If those judges have not the good sense and decency to resign from their positions as judges, they should be removed either by impeachment or by the cote of the decent people of their constituency."[123]

On that note, it is important to remember, in considering the actual breadth of my proposed "non-sexual" or neutral obscenity doctrine, that the third prong would remain intact and thus continue to act as a type of passive "savings clause" for the obscenity doctrine generally.

> "whether the work, taken as a whole, lacks serious literary, artistic, political, or scientific value."

This prong of the *Miller*-test would have increased importance given the expanded scope of the proposed neutral obscenity doctrine. Two examples stemming from express concerns raised by the U.S. Supreme Court in recent First Amendment cases come to mind.

In *Ashcroft v. Free Speech Coalition*, the Majority, in considering the constitutionality of certain aspects of the Child Pornography Prevention Act of 1996, (CPPA) expressed concerns that provisions of the CPPA "prohibits speech despite its serious literary, artistic, political or scientific value." The Court goes on to list examples where the CPPA might ban what are considered to be "serious" works such as Shakespeare's *Romeo and Juliet*, a sexual scene involving a 16-year-old girl in the movie *Traffic*, and various scenes involving teenagers engaged in sexual activity in the movie *American Beauty*. The Court also identifies that the CPPA might criminalize a picture in a "psychology manual."[124]

This is an issue of non-concern with the application of a content-neutral obscenity doctrine. Even if a community might be free, (through its "community standards") due to the level of "super-offensiveness" to find that certain "virtual child pornography" was obscene, (including items or works that would not meet the existing *Miller*-test for obscenity) the existing "third-prong" of *Miller* would continue to be in effect preventing items such as *Romeo and Juliet* and the listed movies from being labeled obscene. Items such as a picture in a psychology manual would also not be deemed offensive due the fact that they would contain serious "scientific" value under the still-viable third prong.

A second example involving the application of the non-sexual obscenity doctrine to obscene "conduct" would be in the instance of cross-burning. The U.S. Supreme Court, in *Virginia v. Black*, expresses concern over "overly-criminalizing" cross burning stating:

> "[O]ccasionally a person who burns a cross does not intend to express a statement of ideology or intimidation. Cross burnings have appeared in movies such as Mississippi Burning, and in plays such as the stage adaptation of Sir Walter Scott's The Lady of the Lake."

Again, a doctrine of non-sexual obscenity that would allow a given community to hold that cross-burning is an obscene act under the proposed standard or test would not endanger such works as *Mississippi Burning* or the adaptation of *The Lady of the Lake* as neither of these items is likely to be found "lacking" in the areas covered by the existing third-prong of *Miller*.

In *Video Software Dealers Assoc. v. Maleng*, the U.S. District Court for the Western District of Washington (at Seattle) provided some explanation for the historical reasoning that obscenity only apply to sexually-explicit materials.

The court explains: "In addition to the fact that the Supreme Court has expressly limited "obscenity" to include only sexually-explicit materials, the historical justifications for the obscenity exception simply do not apply to depictions of violence."[125] This is not a simple distinction.

The court continues:

> Sexually-explicit materials were originally excluded from the protections of the First Amendment because the prevention and punishment of lewd speech has very little, if any, impact on the free expression of ideas and government regulation of the sexually obscene has never been thought to raise constitutional problems.
> …
> The same cannot be said for depictions of violence: such depictions have been used in literature, art, and the media to convey important messages throughout our history, and there is no indication that such expressions have ever been excluded from the protections of the First Amendment or subject to government regulation.[126]

There are so many problems here I will take this in order. First, banning sexually-explicit materials has "little, if any, impact on…free expression." According to whom? It seems that extreme sexual content could be as expressive as extreme violence. I can point to several Supreme Court decisions (including a couple from Justice Black) that would counter this court's assertion that "government regulation of the sexually obscene has <u>never</u> been thought to raise constitutional problems." *Never?*

Violence is used to convey "important" messages? Again, "important" to whom? Can't sex be as "important" as violence? Lastly, the court is being intellectually dishonest. The court asserts that if the obscenity doctrine was content-neutral and materials with extreme violent-content, in certain instances, could be deemed obscene, that the depictions of violence that "have been used in literature, art, and the media to convey important messages throughout our history…" would be endangered. This is nonsense. The third prong of *Miller* would continue to protect explicitly violent material that contained (or did not "lack") "serious literary, artistic, political, or scientific value."

An Additional Miller third "Prong"

A further element of my proposed content-neutral obscenity doctrine would be the addition of an element to the third prong of the existing *Miller*-test. Currently, "the Government must prove that the work, taken as a whole,….lacks serious literary, artistic, political, or scientific value." This prong should be expanded under a content-neutral obscenity doctrine to include "educational…value."

"How's My Driving? Call 1-800-EAT-SHIT!"

"First, for those citizens without wealth or power, a bumper sticker may be one of the few means available to convey a message to a public audience."[127]

"[T]he Court has shown special solicitude for forms of expression that are much less expensive than feasible alternatives and hence may be important to a large segment of the citizenry."[128]

If you don't take at least a few minutes to peruse and survey the merchandise racks at the local gas stations and truck stops across this great land, you are letting one of life's great experiences pass you by. For many, bumper stickers provide a personal and wandering canvas to express their most personally held beliefs. These stickers convey the full-spectrum of political ideology, religious beliefs, humor, satire and even outrage.

One of my favorites cases, *Baker v. Glover*, deals with many issues that surround my proposal of a content-neutral obscenity doctrine (if it is determined that we should have one at all).

Like Ron White, my tattoo-artist friend from South Carolina, Wayne Baker is my kind of First Amendment hero. After learning that trucking companies were placing stickers such as "How's My Driving? Call 1-800-2-ADVISE" on trucks, Baker, in protest to this development, purchased a bumper sticker from a Panama City novelty shop that read, "How's My Driving? Call 1-800-EAT SHIT!" and placed it on his pickup truck.

Baker was stopped by Commander Glover of the Alabama Department of Public Safety and warned that the bumper sticker violated § 13A-12-131 which was Alabama's newly enacted obscenity statute. The statute stated:

> "It shall be unlawful for any person to display in public any bumper sticker, sign or writing which depicts obscene language descriptive of sexual or excretory activities."

Glover threatened Baker with a fine for violation of the statute unless Baker removed the words "eat shit" from the bumper sticker. Glover also informed Baker that the words "crap" or "doo-doo" would violate the statute. Baker agreed to scratch out the offending language and later decided to sue under 42 U.S.C.A. § 1983 asserting that the law violated his First and Fourteenth Amendment rights under the U.S. Constitution.[129]

In *Baker*, the court holds that the bumper sticker does not appeal to the prurient interest of either children or adults. The State of Alabama goes to great lengths to show that this bumper sticker could appeal to the prurient interest of certain "sexual deviants."[130] The State presented "extensive testimony on the subjects of 'coprophilia' (specific fixation upon the products of bodily excretion), 'coprophagy' (erotic interest in consuming fecal excrement), and 'coprolalia' (the uttering of obscenities in order to achieve sexual gratification).[131]

Although the court concedes that, while such deviants do exist, the proper inquiry as to prurient interest assesses a work "in terms of the sexual interests of its intended and probable recipient group."[132]

Beyond finding that the bumper sticker was not 'obscene' due to the fact that a large majority of Alabama's population are not turned on by shit, (close call that it is) the court further held that the bumper sticker was protected "because it has serious literary and political value."[133]

Although surely not a likely candidate for a literary prize, Baker's bumper sticker has *serious literary value* as a parody of stickers such as, "How's My Driving? Call 1-800-2-ADVISE." It and other similar bumper stickers can be compared in many respects to riddles, puns, and proverbs in that they are very short, usually a line or two, and concise in their message. As the Supreme Court has observed "one man's vulgarity is another's lyric." *Cohen*, 403 U.S. at 25, 91 S. Ct. at 1788. Baker's sticker also has *serious political value* as a protest against the "Big Brother" mentality promoted by such other bumper stickers that urge the public to report the indiscretions of truck drivers.[134]

Although I don't believe too many communities would find their community standards violated by Baker's sticker anyway, if we imagine that "prurient interest" was not required initially, instead of not being detected by the court, this case gives us a brief illustration of how the third-prong of *Miller* would act to "save" valuable speech from being deemed obscene under a constitutional framework employing content-neutral or non-sexual obscenity.

Conclusion on Obscenity

"While it is 'obscenity and indecency' before us today, the experience of mankind–both ancient and modern–shows that this type of elastic phrase can, and most likely will, be synonymous with the political and maybe with the religious orthodoxy of tomorrow

...

Censorship is the deadly enemy of freedom and progress. The plain language of the Constitution forbids it. I protest against the Judiciary giving it a foothold here."[135]

I knew that the time had come to question the underlying rationale of the existing obscenity doctrine under *Miller*, including the above proposal for non-sexual obscenity, when I read the following in a recent U.S. Supreme Court case:

"[J]ust as a State may regulate that obscenity which is the most obscene due to its prurient content...."[136] Does this mean that there is obscenity without prurient content?

With this statement it appears that the Court is acknowledging that there is certain obscenity that does not contain prurient content that the State is powerless to regulate and, thus, only that obscenity with a certain level of prurient content can be regulated by the State. This seems to fly in the face of the accepted definition of obscenity under *Miller* that requires prurient content to even be labeled as obscene in the first place.

If it does not, and the Court is acknowledging that the State is only free to regulate that obscenity which is obscene enough, (due to its high level of prurient content?) then implicitly the Court is conceding that the obscenity test under *Miller*, which dictates which materials are to be deemed as obscene for purposes of state restriction, is a content-based determination within a vast range of materials that would commonly be deemed obscene by a lay-person not overly-concerned with Supreme Court balancing tests.

As previously discussed, given the structure of the First Amendment and its express set of commands, the obscenity doctrine is an unwarranted expansion of governmental power by an undemocratic judiciary, ironically taking a drastic step which the representative Congress is expressly forbidden to take. ("Congress shall make no law....")

Alternatively, if the First Amendment *is* to be saddled with "balancing tests" to "balance" an Amendment penned in the strictest of language, the *Miller*-test should not include a sexual or "prurient" requirement which, in effect, creates a content-based "balancing test" to deal with "content-based" speech and speech-expression. However ill-advised and illogical "balancing tests" are within the structure of the First Amendment generally, the least the Court could do is provide balanced "balancing tests."

3

"A-bridging the Gap"

The role of the First Amendment and "Congress[ional] abridg[ment]" in tort suits involving extreme speech and expression.

Does the First Amendment protect us from the Government alone or has its extensive interpretation created an expansive social contract of irresponsibility between private parties?

Introduction

The murders related to the movie *Natural Born Killers* are not only relevant to our discussion of non-sexual obscenity (ch. 2, *above*) but are also highly relevant in discussion related to whether the First Amendment should preclude civil liability in "shock tort" or "copycat" cases where both parties are private citizens and the damages sought are in the form of money damages. *Natural Born Killers* director Oliver Stone commented on this relationship between the First Amendment and the media:

> In the *Natural Born Killers* case here in Louisiana, over the five years of the case, I began to understand that journalists were writing with the presumption that Hollywood people were seeking to hide behind the First Amendment's free speech clauses, while we were really laughing and making money exploiting the public. I find this outrageously cynical. As in any business—yours included [Stone was addressing the annual convention of Alternative News-weeklies in New Orleans] there are always deadbeats, but laws cannot be especially formulated for deadbeats without threatening the wider freedoms of social contract.
>
> But, still, whether anybody is hiding or not is not the issue because the First Amendment *is* the First Amendment. It need not be reinterpreted. And it pro-

tects a lot of assholes, as it does a lot of opinionated right and wrong people. And no excuse needs to be given by me or the producers of *Natural Born Killers*–or anyone for that matter–as to why we express ourselves in the way that we do....[137]

As outlined in the following chapter, Mr. Stone is mistaken in his belief that the First Amendment does not need to be reinterpreted; it does. It must be reinterpreted and brought back to its original designs. He is correct in stating that the First Amendment, as part of the Bill of Rights, is a type of "social contract." He is wrong in believing that this "social contract" should extend to exist between private citizens and not be limited to protecting individuals from the government. He is correct in stating that "no excuse needs to be given...." The collection of money damages in private tort actions between private plaintiffs harmed by the media product of defendants are not about making "excuse[s]." Rather, they are about taking responsibility.

This chapter will examine the role of the First Amendment in private civil tort suits for money damages generally and specifically in the new breed of "shock torts" increasingly filed and litigated in our legal system. Specifically, what is Congressional "abridg[ment]" and does any governmental action, whether by Congress directly or through the courts, that may have the effect of "chilling speech," regardless of how tenuous, invoke the protections of the First Amendment and amount to "Congress[ional]...abridg[ment]" as prohibited under the First Amendment?

Is the Bill of Rights, specifically the First Amendment, a type of social contract between not just the federal government[138] and the people, but also among and between the people themselves?

I. *General Scope of Protection under the First Amendment:*

Originally, the Bill of Rights, including the First Amendment, protected citizens (or in some places, "the People") from the power of the federal government. It was meant to limit the federal government's power over both citizens and states. Over time, the rights guaranteed by the Bill of Rights have been "incorporated" to provide individuals a federalism clause protection from over-expansive state laws. This chapter will examine whether there is any governmental action, or "Congress[ional] abridge[ment], when tort suits that exist between private parties would assign money damages for certain speech and speech-related acts and whether existing First Amendment precedent that deals with situations where the government itself is attempting to suppress speech (*i.e. Brandenburg*) are applicable, in any way, to private tort causes of action.

II.   *The First Amendment in Suits Between Private Parties*

> *The liberty of the press is indeed essential to the nature of a free state, but this consists in laying no previous restraints upon publications, and not in freedom from censure for criminal matters when published. Every free man has an undoubted right to lay what sentiments he pleases before the public; to forbid this is to destroy the freedom of the press; but if he publishes what is improper, mischievous, or illegal, he must take the consequences of his own temerity...*[139]

• Distinguishing *New York Times v. Sullivan*:[140]

Before delving into the specific law and textual references that comprise my argument in this section, it is helpful to review, and distinguish, the Court's 1964 ruling in *New York Times v. Sullivan*.

The most oft-cited outcome of the *New York Times* opinion is that "public official[s]"[141] can only sue for libel for defamation related to official conduct when he or she can prove that the statement was made with "actual malice."[142] *New York Times* is also frequently cited as proof that the First Amendment disallows civil actions that might act, in some capacity, to "chill" speech.[143] This is not so much a mischaracterization of the opinion but more a mistake by the Supreme Court as to the correct reach and scope of the First Amendment.

In *New York Times*, the Court speaks directly to, and then incorrectly dismisses, the Constitutional distinction between state criminal sanction and a tort suit between private parties for money damages. "It matters not that the law has been applied in a civil action and that it is common law only, though supplemented by statute...[t]he test is not the form in which state power has been applied but whatever the form, whether such power has in fact been exercised."[144]

It has become almost instinctual in American culture, legal and otherwise, that the First Amendment is relevant whenever the government, either directly or indirectly, becomes involved as the result of an individual's speech or expression.

The reason for this development is unclear. The First Amendment expressly states "Congress shall make no law...abridging the freedom of speech, or of the press."[145] In order for a complete examination of the role of this Amendment in private torts suits or shock torts, careful examination of the express language of the First Amendment becomes necessary.

a.   *Congress[ional] abridge[ment]*

As an initial matter, it is not clear that "Congress" takes any action, or specifically "abridges" speech in any manner, when one private party brings suit against another for money damages stemming from a "shock tort."

It appears clear that in suits with direct governmental action, the First Amendment prevents "Congress" from enacting a law that would proscribe speech through government interference. For example, in landmark cases such as *Brandenburg, Cohen,*[146] *Chaplinski*[147] and *Miller,*[148] cases that have resulted in the specific legal boundaries of the First Amendment, it is clear that a law enacted by Congress[149] directly "abridge[d]" speech as criminal penalties stemmed from the statute for speech and speech-related conduct.

Clearly, this is not the case in matters where "shock torts" result in tort suits for money damages between private parties.

b.   *...shall make no law...*

The language of the First Amendment prohibits Congress from making certain types of laws. When a court hears a tort case between private litigants what law has been made? It seems clear that the First Amendment is an express restriction on Congress, and its ability to pass laws.

c.   *Judicial Imposition of Judgment and Damages*

Does the simple fact that a court may oversee a trial between private parties or "impose" liability or uphold a jury's verdict constitute governmental action sufficient to mandate the protections of the First Amendment? If so, it appears that the necessary amount of governmental action needed to invoke the First Amendment is broader, and less direct, than the express language of the First Amendment.

The analysis of the District Court in the *Rice v. Paladin Press* lawsuit, already covered in detail provides a glimpse of the general state of the law that requires an express exception to the First Amendment before allowing a lawsuit between private parties to survive summary judgment and proceed to trial where damages could be assigned against the defendant in a cause of action grounded in tort where the government is not a party.

The thought process of the District Court in relation to the lawsuit is telling of the assumed nature of the First Amendment in any lawsuit involving speech:

...the First Amendment would not permit courts to impose liability, no matter what label such a claim carried. In short, however ingenious the attempt to find a side or *back door* that might be opened if the *First Amendment barred the front door to such a liability claim,* the Constitution's *guarantee of free speech and press simply did not allow recovery* of damages for the effects of advocacy or incitement.

It is not clear why damages stemming from a private tort suit would constitute a "back door" approach in relation to the protections of the First Amendment. Specifically, what does the First Amendment have to do with the recovery of damages? Are damages reached in the course of a private lawsuit where the government is not a party shielded by the First Amendment generally on the presumption that they might "chill" speech? It is clear that the government could not directly proscribe speech that does not fall under one of the express exceptions of the First Amendment, as interpreted (in this case, inciting imminent lawless activity under *Brandenburg*) and, as this is the case, the government could not, for example, seize the book *Hit Man* from the shelves, outlaw its sale, arrest buyers of the book, or take any other direct action that might actually reach the level of governmental "abdidg[ment]." But, in the opinion, *above,* the district court determines that the outer boundaries of the "guarantee[s] of free speech..." include not just the guarantee to be free from governmental restriction (or "Congress[ional] abridge[ment]") but also the guarantee to be protected from any *and all liability* towards other individuals, in effect transforming the Bill of Rights and the First Amendment into a social contract not just between individuals and their government, but also a social contract between citizens themselves.

III.   *Libel, Slander and actions in Tort that show an existing balance between tort law and the First Amendment*

The controlling thesis of this section seems less dramatic when viewed in light of the existing legal framework that governs defamation-based tort claims for libel and slander. Existing law surrounding the First Amendment and tort lawsuits allows plaintiffs a great deal more latitude to recover money damages for injuries to reputation as opposed to the recovery of money damages for other types of harm proximately linked to a defendant.

The right to legal redress in the civil courts for harm done to an individual's reputation is deeply rooted in Anglo-American jurisprudence.[150] Justice Potter Stewart noted that, "[t]he right of a man to the protection of his own reputation from unjustified invasion and wrongful hurt reflects no more than our basic concept of the essential dignity and worth of every human being–a concept at the root of any decent system of ordered liberty."[151] It appears clear that the "right" Justice Stewart refers to protect his reputation against harm done by other individuals is not thwarted by the existence of the First Amendment.

What makes the more relaxed standard for defamation somewhat ironic in this context is the direct nature between the tort cause of action and the speech at issue. In libel and slander cases, the defamation-based causes of action are specifically aimed at speech. In other, more general negligence or tort lawsuits, the cause of action is not inherently aimed at speech.

IV. The Mis-Application of Brandenburg to Private Tort Suits:
a. Overview of Brandenburg

To understand why the theories and rules set forth in *Brandenburg* and it progeny are *mis*-applied in private tort suits a general understanding of the landmark decision is necessary.[152]

In *Brandenburg*, the U.S. Supreme Court, in a *per curium* decision, reversed the conviction of Clarence Brandenburg, the leader of a Ku Klux Klan (KKK) group, who had previously been convicted under Ohio's Criminal Syndicalism law.[153] Mr. Brandenburg was sentenced to 1 to 10 years imprisonment and fined $1,000. The Court held that the law violated the First Amendment and could not be sustained because it punished "mere advocacy" and the "assembly with others merely to advocate the described type of action." The lasting effect of *Brandenburg*, generally, is that the incitement of imminent lawless action can be constitutionally proscribed and punished, whereas the "mere advocacy" of unlawful actions or activities is protected by the First Amendment.

b. General mis-application of Brandenburg

The standard or "test" set forth by *Brandenburg* appears to be a workable, and overall logical approach to assigning boundaries for governmental interference in free-speech related to unlawful actions or activities. That it is inapplicable in situations between private parties does not diminish from or argue against its validity in situations where the government acts directly to proscribe, prevent or interfere with speech or speech-conduct.

One aspect of the constitutional test set forth under *Brandenburg* evidences the manner that it is inapplicable to private tort lawsuits. The crucial distinction reached by the Court in *Brandenburg*, whether an individual "merely advocates" illegal activity or "incites imminent lawless action," is practically irrelevant to the law surrounding "shock tort" lawsuits.

C.   *Addressing the Kunich proposed "New Alternative" to Brandenburg*

In his 2000 article published in the WASHINGTON UNIVERSITY LAW QUARTERLY, *Natural Born Copycat Killers and the Law of Shock Torts*, Professor John Charles Kunich addresses the inapplicability of *Brandenburg* to speech-related "shock torts" defined by Kunich as:

> ...a cause of action based on acts of violence causally linked to the perpetrator's exposure–especially if a minor–to shockingly violent forms of mass entertainment that, on their face, appear to be calculated primarily to appear to persons with an appetite for killing or sociopathic behavior particularly of an unlawful nature.[154]

Kunich proposes an alternative to the general use of *Brandenburg* for situations involving shock torts. The Kunich approach is worthy of examination and appears to constitute a middle-ground between the common application of *Brandenburg* and the perceived necessity of an express exception to First Amendment protections in order that this type of shock tort lawsuit survive, and the thesis of this article that the First Amendment does not constitute any barrier to tort suits between private parties for money damages.

Kunich's approach is expressed in a somewhat "Learned Hand" fashion, distilling and summarizing a legal "test" in a mathematical and abbreviated format:[155]

$$V \Leftrightarrow M \times P \times B$$

Briefly, **V** is the **"value"** of the speech, **M** is the **"magnitude"** of resultant physical harm, **P** is the **"probability"** of physical harm ensuing from the speech, and **B** is the degree to which the **"balance"** of hardships favors the plaintiff.[156]

An exhaustive review of Kunich's approach is outside of the scope of this section; it would serve readers interested in this area of the intersection of First Amendment and tort law well to read Kunich's excellent article.[157]

Specifically, Kunich's approach is predicated on the acceptance that finding liability for certain shock torts must be found inside the boundaries of the enumerated First Amendment exception for "incitement."[158] Kunich introduces the V ⇔ M x P x B test with an express acceptance of the Constitutional pigeonhole created by *Brandenburg*:

> Although not meant to supplant *Brandenburg* in all cases, this alternative test should rework the Brandenburg analytical framework to address more appropriately the particular factual and legal features that prevail in the shock torts context and related situations. Specifically, courts should use the test when some physical harm has allegedly resulted from mass-media speech, *and the only avenue of redress in light of the First Amendment is some form of incitement.*[159]

The entire necessity of Kunich's alternative approach is cured, in effect, by the application of the thesis of this chapter, that the First Amendment does not impede private torts suits to the degree acknowledged and accepted by Kunich and therefore the application of a *"Brandenburg* alternative" becomes unnecessary. This article theorizes that the general acceptance (embodied in the language, "in light of the First Amendment," *above*) that the First Amendment restricts private tort lawsuits is not valid as no governmental action, generally, or "Congress[ional] abridge[ment]," specifically, is present.[160]

d. *Rice v. Paladin Press as a study in the mis-application of Brandenburg:*

In 1997 the United States Court of Appeals for the Fourth Circuit, in a unanimous ruling, allowed the pivotal case *Rice v. Paladin Press* to survive a First Amendment defense by publisher Paladin Press, stay alive beyond summary judgment, and proceed to trial.[161] The case settled on the eve of trial and a jury never heard the lurid details of the instruction manual that helped James Perry murder three people in a cross-country murder-for-hire scheme. *Rice v. Paladin Enterprises* remains a landmark case because of its ruling which allows a plaintiff to sue a publisher solely for what is published in written form.

The First Amendment argument at both the district court and the Fourth Circuit Court of Appeals was whether the publishing of the book *Hit Man: A Tech-*

nical Manual for Independent Contractors by Paladin Press, a Colorado-based mail order publishing company, amounted to the incitement of imminent lawless action under the standard and First Amendment-test set forth under *Brandenburg v. Ohio*. The book contained step-by-step instructions on how to carry out a "hit" and kill a "mark" for money. Prior to murdering three people, James Perry, a convicted felon from Detroit, followed twenty-two steps directly from the manual that he had ordered from Paladin Press. The district court held that the book did not meet the standard set forth in *Brandenburg*, and therefore did not meet the enumerated exception for speech which incites imminent lawless action and thus place it outside the general protections of the First Amendment. The Fourth Circuit reversed holding that the First Amendment does not provide an absolute bar to recovery for the Plaintiffs and did not mandate summary dismissal. The Fourth Circuit remanded the case back to the district court for trial.

While *Brandenburg* would, at first glance, appear to be the correct and applicable standard under the First Amendment, numerous distinctions lie in the facts of both the situation that gave rise to the *Paladin Enterprises* lawsuit and the nature of the lawsuit itself, that drastically alter the role of the First Amendment in private civil suits for money damages, (*i.e. Paladin Enterprises*) differently than suits where the government has taken direct steps to proscribe the speech or expression at issue. (*i.e. Brandenburg*)

i.   The Fourth Circuit's Analysis of the District Court's misunderstanding of Brandenburg:

The District Court held that "*Hit Man* is entitled to the protections of *Brandenburg* in any event because it is a mere instructional manual for, and not an incitement to, murder."[162] The Fourth Circuit held that the District Court's analysis of *Brandenburg* was in error because the lower court had interpreted *Brandenburg* to "protect not just abstract advocacy of lawlessness…but also the teaching of the technical methods of criminal activity—in this case, the technical methods of murder."[163]

The Fourth Circuit views this type of "teaching" to be closer to the immediate incitement of lawlessness than to the abstract advocacy of it, in this case finding that Paladin's publishing the book amounted to civil aiding and abetting under Maryland law.

Hit Man moves past mere "abstract advocacy," which would seemingly include abstractly encouraging that criminal activity take place, to actually assisting an individual through a detailed, step-by-step manual, on how to commit the particular crime. In providing this "assistance," in which the actual speech itself is the criminal act, history makes it clear that the First Amendment provides no protection for this type of criminal activity.

The court acknowledges that the state is free to proscribe and punish numerous crimes that are, in many cases, wholly acts of speech:

> Were the First Amendment to bar or to limit government regulation of such "speech brigaded with action," the government would be powerless to protect the public from countless of even the most pernicious criminal acts and civil wrongs.[164]

The court then goes on to list specific examples of this type of criminal and civil act: extortion or blackmail, threats and other improper influences in official and political matters, perjury and various cognate crimes, criminal solicitation, threatening the life of the President, conspiracy, harassment, forgery, successfully soliciting another to commit suicide, and false public alarms.[165]

ii. Further analysis of the mis-application of Brandenburg under alternative theory of "shock tort" liability

While there are several reasons that *Brandenburg* is being mis-applied within existing First Amendment jurisprudence, here I will specifically outline why *Brandenburg* is inapplicable in "shock tort" cases for money damages involving private parties. When imposed, the *Brandenburg* standard acts as an absolute bar, in most cases, to the progress of the tort lawsuit. The First Amendment's original design does not mandate that doctrines such as *Brandenburg* be applied in situations between private parties that do not directly involve the government in any way.

> "A shock tort is a cause of action based on acts of violence causally linked to the perpetrator's exposure—especially if a minor—to shockingly violent forms of mass entertainment…"[166]

Many "shock tort" cases take the form of "copycat" crimes in which individuals emulate the different forms of "mass entertainment." Courts have generally dealt with the relationship between works of mass entertainment and criminal activity by applying *Brandenburg*. In most cases, the application of this First Amendment test has functioned as an absolute bar to the progression of the "shock tort" suit.

Shock tort cases should live or die under tort law. Given that the government is not directly involved in the case, the First Amendment, which prohibits only Congress[ional] abridge[ment] of speech and of the press is generally inapplicable. My assertion is that the framework of tort law is a sufficient forum for these cases and the First Amendment should not function as an absolute bar in disputes arising between private parties.

Transitioning very briefly from the First Amendment to the Second Amendment, an individual may well have a Constitutional right to bear arms. Regardless, if an individual uses a firearm in a negligent, intentional or reckless manner, the Second Amendment does not serve as an absolute bar to tort suits between private parties. The First Amendment is not meant to protect citizens from one another. Even in cases where money damages are awarded to a private party this does not necessarily mean that this individual can no longer "speak;" it simply means that through tort actions, society has shifted certain burdens between its members.

As discussed more fully in the section below, the Fourth Circuit commented on the difficulty in successfully litigating such a suit even when the First Amendment does not act as an absolute bar on liability.[167]

> [I]n contrast to the case before us, in virtually every "copycat" case, there will be lacking in the speech itself any basis for a permissible inference that the "speaker" intended to assist and facilitate the criminal conduct described or depicted. Of course, with few, if any, exceptions, the speech which gives rise to the copycat crime will not directly and affirmatively promote the criminal conduct, even if, in some circumstances, it incidentally glamorizes and thereby indirectly promotes such conduct.

The "Soldier of Fortune" mini-Circuit-Split

A short line of cases that sheds further light on the application and evolution of the intersection First Amendment analysis within the framework of private tort cases is found in three cases involving the use of classified magazine ads to recruit individuals to commit crimes. Although the facts in two of the cases were quite similar, two federal circuit courts differed in their handling of the "incitement" standard within the framework of a civil tort lawsuit.

Eimann v. Soldier of Fortune Magazine

The following classified ad ran in the September, October and November 1984 issues of *Soldier of Fortune* magazine:

> **"EX-MARINES–67-69 'Nam Vets, Ex DI, weapons specialist–jungle warfare, pilot, M.E. high risk assignments, U.S. or overseas. (404) 991-2684"[168]**

Through this ad, John Wayne Hearn was contacted by Robert Black, a man who had been searching for some time to find someone to kill his wife Sandra.[169] Following the murder, Sandra Black's family sued *Soldier of Fortune* ("*SOF*") magazine and its parent, Omega Group, Ltd., for wrongful death under Texas law on the theory that *SOF* had acted negligently in published Hearn's classified ad.[170]

The court held that under the Texas risk-utility balancing test, *SOF* magazine did not violate the required standard of conduct and was, therefore, not liable under a theory of negligent publication. The court expressly declined to address any type of First Amendment claim, instead relying on "general negligence principles":

> We need not address SOF's first amendment attacks on the judgment to resolve this appeal. Assuming without deciding that a Texas court would apply general negligence principles to this case, we conclude that no liability can attach under these principles as a matter of law. SOF owed no duty to refrain from publishing a facially innocuous classified advertisement when the ad's context–at most–made the message ambiguous.[171]

Braun v. Soldier of Fortune Magazine

The following classified ad ran in the June 1985 through March 1986 issues of *Soldier of Fortune* magazine:

> **"GUN FOR HIRE: 37 year old professional mercenary desires jobs. Vietnam Veteran. Discrete [sic] and very private. Body guard, courier, and other special skills. All jobs considered. Phone (615) 436-9785 (days) or (615) 436-4335 (nights), or write: Rt. 2 Box 682 Village Loop Road, Gatlinburg, TN 37738."[172]**

Through this ad, Michael Savage was contacted by Bruce Gastwirth, who wanted to have his business partner, Richard Braun, murdered. Following the murder, Gastwirth's family sued *SOF* for wrongful death similarly alleging that the magazine had been negligent in running the ad.

Prior to hiring Savage, Gastwirth had arranged for three unsuccessful previous attempts on Braun's life. On August 26, 1985, Savage, Moore [another individual enlisted by Gastwirth] and another individual, Sean Trevor Doutre, went to Braun's house in the Atlanta suburbs. As Braun and his teenage son were driving down the driveway, Doutre stepped in front of the car and fired several shots at the car with a MAC 11 automatic pistol. The shots hit both Braun and his son, Michael. After being shot, Braun managed to roll out of the car where Doutre subsequently murdered him execution-style by firing two more shots into the back of his head.

Braun involved the interpretation of Georgia law by the district court sitting in Alabama. The court held that under Georgia law, for a party to prevail in an action for negligence, it must establish the following elements:

1. A legal duty to conform to a standard of conduct raised by the law for the protection of others against unreasonable risks of harm;

2. [A] breach of this standard;

3. [A] legally attributable causal connection between the conduct and the resulting injury; and

4. [S]ome loss or damage flowing to the plaintiff's legally protected interest as a result of the alleged breach of the legal duty.

The court noted that once a legal duty is found to exist, "it generally leaves for the jury issues of negligence and proximate cause."[173] Under Georgia law, the court applied a risk-utility analysis and held that "the district court properly found that SOF had a legal duty to refrain from publishing advertisements that subjected the public, including appellees, to a clearly identifiable unreasonable risk of harm from violent criminal activity."[174]

Although the outcomes in the two cases, *Eimann* and *Braun*, were dissimilar, the court expressly distinguishes the two:

SOF's reliance on *Eimann* is misplaced. We distinguish *Eimann* from this case based on the instructions to the respective juries. In *Eimann*, the district court violated risk-utility balancing principles when it allowed the jury to impose liability on SOF if a reasonable publisher would conclude "that the advertisement *could reasonably be interpreted*" as an offer to commit crimes. 880 F.2d at 833 (emphasis added). The Fifth Circuit correctly observed that virtually anything *might* involve illegal activity, id. at 837, and that applying the district court's standard would mean that a publisher "must reject *all* [ambiguous] advertisements," *id.* at 838 (emphasis in original), or risk liability for any "untoward consequences that flow from his decision to publish" them, *id.*

Regardless of the outcome of the cases, respectively, it does appear that a general negligence, risk-utility analysis can provide a proper and workable framework for courts to consider and juries to apply.[175]

Norwood v. Soldier of Fortune Magazine, Inc.[176]

The following classified ads ran during 1985 in *SOF* magazine:

> **GUN FOR HIRE: 37 year-old-professional mercenary desires jobs. Vietnam Veteran. Discreet and very private. Bodyguard, courier, and other special skills. All jobs considered. Phone (615) 891-3306 (I-03).** [ad for Savage]; and

> **GUN FOR HIRE. NAM sniper instructor. SWAT. Pistol, rifle, security specialist, bodyguard, courier plus. All jobs considered. Privacy guaranteed. Mike (214) 756-5941 (101)** [ad for Jackson].

While not directly relevant to the present examination of these cases as related to the "incitement doctrine," a 1990 *WASHINGTON & LEE LAW REVIEW* article distinguished this type of "gun-for-hire" advertisement from other types of protected speech:

> This issue does not revolve around political speech, as in *New York Times Co.* v. or even fiction and drama as in *Olivia N. v. National Broadcasting Co.* Instead, the speech involved in the hired gun cases is quintessential commercial speech, "which does no more than propose a commercial transaction."[177]

The court's opinion, in *Norwood*, goes to the heart of the distinction between government involvement and money damages between individuals stating:

"It should be pointed out that, even though defendant argues, and plaintiff seems to agree, that this is a case in which the court has to determine whether the 'speech' exercised by the defendant can be regulated to any degree, the court simply does not believe that that is the issue. Mr. Norwood is not attempting to have defendant enjoined from exercising its right to run advertisements such as those in question. Instead, he is simply asking that a jury, after a trial, award him damages for the consequences of those advertisements. Thus, the cases cited by both plaintiff and defendant on the permissible boundaries of regulation of First Amendment rights simply do not apply."[178]

The court also rejects, as I have, an overly-broad reading of *New York Times v. Sullivan* holding:

If this court were to accept the argument of [SOF], it is obvious that it would take the Sullivan holding far beyond the intended result. Defendant contends that its 'gun for hire' advertisements are absolutely privileged. The court understands that to mean that, irrespective of how a jury might view defendant's alleged conduct in this case, the First Amendment still will not allow the plaintiff to expect the defendant to answer in damages for its conduct. That simply cannot be the law, and the court does not believe that *Sullivan, supra,* and *Rosenblatt, supra,* can be stretched to the point argued by defendant, even in a 'public official case' such as those two cases were, and certainly not in a 'commercial speech' case.[179]

Suicidal Porn–the "Orgasm of Death" Article

In *Herceg v. Hustler Magazine, Inc.,*[180] the Fifth Circuit considered whether "the publisher of a magazine may be held liable for civil damages."[181] The August 1981 issue of *Hustler* included, as part of a series about pleasurable but sometimes dangerous taboo sexual practices, an article entitled "Orgasm of Death." The article discussed the practice of autoerotic asphyxia which consists of masturbating while "'hanging' oneself in order to temporarily cut off the blood supply to the brain at the moment of orgasm."[182]

The article chronicled both the dangers and the apparent sexual pleasure that can be derived from autoerotic asphyxia. The editor's included a type of disclaimer at the beginning of the article that stated:

"Hustler emphasizes the often-fatal dangers of the practice of 'auto-erotic asphyxia,' and recommends that readers seeking unique forms of sexual release DO NOT ATTEMPT this method. The facts are presented here solely for educational purpose."

Regardless of any warning, a fourteen year old boy attempted the practice after reading the article. The next morning his nude body was found hanging in the closet by a close friend. He was dead. Near the hanging corpse, a copy of the *Hustler* magazine was found open to the "Orgasm of Death" article. The Fifth Circuit, applying the Supreme Court's incitement standard, held that "no liability can attach to *Hustler's* publication of "Orgasm of Death," and therefore *Hustler* was not civilly liable.

While the Circuit opinion is unremarkable given the current state of First Amendment jurisprudence, the dissent in this case foreshadows many of this chapter's assertions with regards to the general inapplicability of the incitement doctrine to tort suits involving money damages.

Circuit Judge Edith Jones, dissenting in part, writes:

> What disturbs me to the point of despair is the majority's broad reasoning which appears to foreclose the possibility that any state might choose to temper the excesses of the pornography business by imposing civil liability for harms it directly causes. Consonant with the first amendment, the state can protect its citizens against the moral evil of obscenity, the threat of civil disorder or injury posed by lawless mobs and fighting words, and the damage to reputation from libel or defamation, to say nothing of the myriad dangers lurking in "commercial speech." Why cannot the state then fashion a remedy to protect its children's lives when they are endangered by suicidal pornography? To deny this possibility, I believe, is to degrade the free market of ideas to a level with the black market for heroin.[183]

Judge Jones finds that the framework of defamation law which allows for the recovery of money damages is analogous to the analysis involved in the collection of money damages for the "Orgasm of Death" article. Judge Jones also holds that by the defamation standard, "both *Hustler* in general and "Orgasm of Death" in particular deserve limited only first amendment protection." The Judge outlines numerous reasons that equating the "speech" contained in Hustler magazine within the existing framework of defamation "hardly portends the end of participatory democracy, as some might contend."

1. "[A]ny given issue of Hustler may be found legally obscene and therefore entitled to no first amendment protection.";

2. "[T]ort liability would result after-the-fact, not as a prior restraint, and would be based on harm directly caused by the publication in issue.";

3.   "[T]o the extent any chilling effect existing from the exposure to tort liability, this would, in my view, protect society from loss of life and limb, a legitimate, indeed compelling, state interest."

4.   "[O]bscenity has been widely regulated by prior restraint for over a century."

Ozzy Osbourne–mistaken interpretation in earlier "shock tort" cases

Long before American voyeurs became fascinated with Ozzy Osbourne's highly dysfunctional home-life, Ozzy's music gave rise to several early "shock tort" suits.

On October 26, 1984, nineteen year old John McCollum shot himself with a .22 caliber handgun after repeatedly listening to Ozzy Osbourne's albums *Blizzard of Oz*, "*Diary of a Madman*" and "*Speak of the Devil*." He was found still wearing the stereo headphones, the needle still riding the inside of the album, the turntable still rotating.

McCollum's family filed a lawsuit against Osbourne alleging that "Osbourne's music was a proximate cause of John's suicide…." Although John McCollum was actually listening to "Speak of the Devil" when he took his life, it is the lyrics of "Suicide Solution," a song that he had previously listened to, that give rise to the lawsuit.

> Wine is fine but whiskey's quicker
> Suicide is slow with liquor
> Take a bottle drown your sorrows
> Then it floods away tomorrows
>
> Evil thoughts and evil doings
> Cold, alone you hand in ruins
> Thought that you'd escape the reaper
> You can't escape the Master Keeper
> Cause you feel life's unreal and you're living a lie
> Such a shame who's to blame and you're wondering why
> Then you ask from your cask is there life after birth
> What you sow can mean Hell on this earth

Now you live inside a bottle
The reaper's traveling at full throttle
It's catching you but you don't see
The reaper is you and the reaper is me

Breaking law, knocking doors
But there's no one at home
Made your bed, rest your head
But you lie there and moan Where to hide,
Suicide is the only way out
Don't you know what it's really about

Ah know people
You really know where its at
You got it
Why try, why try
Get the gun and try it
Shoot, shoot, shoot.

The two-part "Discussion" section of the California Court of Appeal's decision seems tailor-made for our purposes here. The first part, entitled, "The First Amendment Bars Plaintiffs' Action" intelligently and comprehensively outlines the existing law surrounding the First Amendment and mass media and discusses policy reasons that, while valid, do not necessarily invoke the First Amendment to the degree the court recognized.

> The scope of such protection is not limited to merely serving as a bar to the prior restraint of such speech, but also prevents the assertion of a claim for civil damages. "[T]he fear of damage awards…may be markedly more inhibiting than the fear of prosecution under a criminal statute." (*New York Times v. Sullivan* (1964) 376 U.S. 254, 277, 84 S. Ct. 710, 724, 11 L.Ed.2d 686, 704.) Musical composers and performers, as well as record producers and distributors, would become significantly more inhibited in the selection of controversial materials if liability for civil damages were a risk to be endured for publication of protected speech. The deterrent effect of subjecting the music and recording industry to such liability because of their programming choices would lead to a self-censorship which would dampen the vigor and limit the variety of artistic expression. Thus, the imposition here of post publication

> civil damages, in the absence of an incitement to imminent lawless action, would be just as violative of the First Amendment as a prior restraint.[184]

In the above paragraph the court mistakenly defines the boundaries of the First Amendment on admirable policy demands. It may be true that the "fear of damage awards" may well inhibit free speech more than "prosecution under a criminal statute," but this fact alone does not mean that the two are identical under the First Amendment. The text of the First Amendment directly speaks to "prosecution under a criminal statute" because this is the result of "Congress" making a law that may abridge free speech. The First Amendment is absolutely silent on the issue of civil awards stemming from an action between two private parties. Simply because the fear exists does not mean that it is remedied by the First Amendment.

Similarly, the fear of civil damages causing those in the music programming business to self-censor is also a legitimate fear in a free society. Nonetheless, even if this should be avoided, the First Amendment does not demand that these damages not be allowed because of this indirect effect.

Finally, the court states that "imposition here of post publication civil damages, in the absence of an incitement to imminent lawless action, would be just as violative of the First Amendment as a prior restraint." Why? The *Brandenburg* standard to which the court refers is relevant in situations where the government directly prohibits speech through criminal prosecution. A prior restraint where the government curtails speech directly runs afoul of the First Amendment in almost every case. It is unclear why civil damages in a case between two private parties is "just as violative of the First Amendment" as a prior restraint.

The second part of the "Discussion" section, titled "The First Amendment Bar Aside, Plaintiffs Have Alleged No Basis for Recovery of Damages," is illustrative of a second important principle: Regardless of whether the First Amendment serves as an absolute bar to civil recovery, the general rules of tort provide a workable and adequate framework for civil claims made against extreme speech.

The court analyzed Osbourne's civil liability under general principles of negligence and tort. Finding that the suicide was not foreseeable and that Osbourne didn't have the necessary "intent" to be held liable, the court dismissed the case. The court also correctly identified the legitimate reluctance by courts to hold artists liable for speech that may "adversely affect emotionally troubled individuals":[185]

"Finally, and perhaps most significantly, it is simply not acceptable to a free and democratic society to impose a duty upon performing artists to limit and restrict their creativity in order to avoid the dissemination of ideas in artistic speech which may adversely affect emotionally troubled individuals."[186]

Clearly, civil liability could have a "chilling" effect on artistic speech. Whether the First Amendment serves as an absolute bar in these cases is unclear. When a private party sues another private party and is awarded money damages has "Congress" made a "law" that chills ("abridges") speech? No. The expansion of the First Amendment from its limited designs to a roving protector of speech in all its forms is expansive and possibly desirable. Regardless, these boundaries should be constructed by Democratic government and not defined by the interpretative arm of courts.

iii.   Paladin Enterprises as "shock tort" precedent

There is little doubt from the large amount of text imported into the court's opinion, and the manner in which the court refers to *Hit Man*, that the decision was, in large part, a reaction to the specific nature, content and tone of the book itself. In the very first footnote, the court explains that even in the inclusion of the passages of *Hit Man* in the opinion "…the court has even felt it necessary to omit portions of these few illustrative passages in order to minimize the danger to the public from their repetition herein."[187]

Surrounding the Paladin Enterprises case was an aura of fear from the First Amendment and media communities. For example, an *amicus* brief filed in the suit asserted:

Allowing this lawsuit to survive [summary judgment] will disturb decades of First Amendment jurisprudence and jeopardize free speech from the periphery to the core…[n]o expression–music, video, books, even newspaper articles– would be safe from civil liability.

The court, highly aware of the fear of its decision, specifically addresses these concerns in its opinion, primarily by pointing out the unique nature of the work in question, in addition to the somewhat "astonishing" stipulations made by Paladin as to its intentions in publishing and marketing the book. Understanding *Paladin's* place as precedent in the shock tort arena, necessitates a quick review of these stipulations.

The Fourth Circuit summarized these stipulations in its opinion:

a. For purposes of summary judgment, Paladin stipulated that "Perry followed…instructions from Hit Man…in planning, executing, and attempting to cover up the murders of Mildred and Trevor Horn and Janice Saunders;[188]

b. Paladin stipulated that "in marketing Hit Man, Paladin 'intended to attract and assist criminals and would be criminals who desire information and instructions on how to commit crimes'….";[189] and

c. Paladin stipulated "it 'intended *and* had knowledge' that Hit Man would actually 'would be used, *upon receipt,* by criminals and would be criminals to plan and execute the crime of murder for hire.'"[190]

In finding that these stipulations were, in themselves, somewhat unusual, the court explained that its ruling would primarily provide precedent only in cases where such similar stipulations were made or such strong actual intent could be derived and presented to the jury. The court found this highly unlikely in almost any subsequent case that might attempt to rely on the *Paladin* decision.

> …there will almost never be evidence proffered from which a jury even could reasonably conclude that the producer or publisher possessed the actual intent to assist criminal activity. In only the rarest cases, as here where the publisher has stipulated in almost taunting defiance that it intended to assist murderers and other criminals, will there be evidence extraneous to the speech itself which would support a finding of the requisite intent; surely few will, as Paladin has, "stand up and proclaim to the world that because they are publishers they have a unique constitutional right to aid and commit [crime].[191]

4

The "Abstract Line" Analysis under Brandenburg

The preceding chapter has outlined the deficiencies in applying *Brandenburg* as the First Amendment standard in a variety of "shock tort" lawsuits between two private parties for money damages. This chapter discusses the need to clarify the "incitement" standard set forth under *Brandenburg* and limit it to its intended "abstract" scope.[192]

In *Brandenburg*, the Supreme Court held that abstract advocacy of lawlessness is protected speech under the First Amendment "so long as the speech is not directed to inciting or producing imminent lawless action and is not likely to incite or produce such action."[193]

It seems that the limits of the test set forth in *Brandenburg* can be gauged by viewing not the actual speech itself, but the reaction of either a certain individual or audience or some third party upon hearing the "message." If the uttering of certain words would cause an immediate hostile reaction from a listener or by their very "utterance inflict injury or tend to incite an immediate breach of the peace" then they could be prohibited as "fighting words." If a reasonable individual would believe that an individual hearing the speech would "believe he will be subjected to physical violence upon his person" then the speech could be proscribed as a "true threat."

Thus, a gray area between protected speech under *Brandenburg* and unprotected speech under other related exceptions to the First Amendment results. In attempting to categorize the void between *Brandenburg* and the outer edges of exceptions such as "fighting words" and "true threats," the common denominator seems to focus on the "abstract" nature of protected speech under *Brandenburg* and later in cases such as *Hess* and *Claiborne*.

…that the mere abstract teaching of **, including the teaching of the moral propriety or even moral necessity for a resort to force and violence, is not the same as preparing a group for violent action and steeling it to such action.[194]

The standard set forth under *Brandenburg* should be limited in its scope to situations where only "mere [abstract] advocacy" is under criminal scrutiny.[195] As indicated by earlier precedent, the distinction between what should and should not fall under the protections of the First Amendment is related to the "remote[ness]" of the speech to the resulting action, it is, as the Court expressed in *Schenck v. United States*, "a question of proximity and degree."[196]

In *Brandenburg*, the racist ranting of the Klan leader did not "steel" anyone to action; although disgusting and utterly without social value, it was a classic example of "abstract" advocacy.

> 'How far is the nigger going to–yeah.'
> 'This is what we are going to do to the niggers.'
> 'A dirty nigger'
> 'Send the Jews back to Israel.'
> 'Let's give them back to the dark garden.'
> 'Save America.'
> 'Let's go back to constitutional betterment.'
> 'Bury the niggers.' 'We intent to do our part.'
> 'Give us our state rights.'
> 'Freedom for the whites.'
> 'Nigger will have to fight for every inch he gets from now on.'[197]

Similarly, in *Hess v. Indiana*, the Court overturned a disorderly conduct conviction of an individual who yelled "[w]e'll take the fucking street later (or again)" as part of anti-war protest.[198]

The Abstract Line Model

Ideas (expressed) <————————A————————> Overt Acts

Some of the most confusing, and controversial, aspects of First Amendment jurisprudence exist in the area between "ideas" and "overt acts."

> *"The line between what is permissible and not subject to control and what may be made impermissible and subject to regulation is the line between ideas and overt acts...[t]he example usually given by those who would punish speech is the case of one who falsely shouts fire in a crowded theatre."*[199]

"Falsely shouting fire in a crowded theatre" is an overworked, but valuable, analogy in First Amendment law. Shouting anything in a crowded theater is likely to get you thrown out of the theater or, if one persists, an arrest for disturbing the peace or disorderly conduct. What is punishable is the effect of the speech on third parties, here the theater patrons. As Justice Douglas continued in his concurrence in *Brandenburg*, "[shouting fire in a crowded theatre] is, however, a classic case where speech is brigaded with action...[t]hey [the speech and action] are indeed inseparable and a prosecution can be launched for the overt acts actually caused."[200] So, where speech that is so closely related to the resulting overt acts as to be deemed "inseparable," the law basically views the words, themselves, to be part of the overt criminal act that can clearly be criminalized.

The Boundaries of "Abstract" Advocacy

Returning to our figurative line of abstraction, and acknowledging that speech that is synonymous with "overt action" can be punished, while "abstract" advocacy of lawless action cannot, *it is the level of abstraction that is this line*. While it appears that most of the *Brandenburg* analysis in this context considers the level of "incitement," it is actually the level of abstraction that is the more relevant inquiry. If the speech at issue is not sufficiently "abstract," then our figurative line diminishes to the point that the "speech" and "overt action" meet. When this occurs, the First Amendment provides no protection for this speech because, at least legally and constructively, it melds into the "overt action" and can be punished as such.

Ideas(e) < [degree of the "*abstract*" nature of the speech] > Overt Acts

Therefore, it is the degree of the "abstract" nature of speech that must be analyzed to attempt to clarify the existing void left by the Court's short *per curium* opinion in *Brandenburg* as to the boundaries of the freedoms of speech and expression. I will apply this analysis to the Fourth Circuit's opinion in *Rice v. Paladin Enterprises, Inc.* to illustrate this analysis.

Rice v Paladin Enterprises, Inc.

In reversing the District Court's opinion, the Fourth Circuit expressly held that the lower court had misunderstood and misapplied *Brandenburg*.

> [I]n this conclusion the district court erred, as well, misunderstanding the Supreme Court's decision in Brandenburg to protect not just abstract advocacy of lawlessness and the open criticism of government and its institutions, but also the teaching of the technical methods of criminal activity–in this case, the technical methods of murder.

Specifically, the court held that "*Hit Man* is, pure and simple, a step-by-step murder manual, a training book for assassins." The court then limits *Brandenburg* to its original design and distinguishes between "mere abstract teaching" (and "mere advocacy") and the type of instructional teaching that is found in *Hit Man*. In *Brandenburg*, the Court held that "the mere abstract teaching...of the moral propriety or even moral necessity" of resorting to lawlessness is protected under the First Amendment.

Returning to our line, the following is an illustration of "abstract" advocacy or teaching that would clearly be protected under *Brandenburg*:

Ideas(e)-> [abstract teaching]—*———————A———————> Overt Acts**
Does not prepare or
"steel" an individual to action

Here, it seems clear that the teaching of "moral propriety" or even "moral necessity" is teaching people the ideas that underlie lawless action and not providing them with the specific information that would immediately incite or "steel" them to action. In relation to the inclusion of ideas and the book, the court finds that "[i]deas simply are neither the focus or burden" of *Hit Man*.

Appellants/Plaintiffs in the *Rice* case asserted a similar theme in their brief:

> *Hit Man* is not political manifesto, not revolutionary diatribe, not propaganda, advocacy, or protest, not an outpouring of conscience or credo.

...

> It contains no discussion of ideas, no argument, no information about politics, religion, science, art, or culture...it offers no agenda for self-governance, no insight into the issues of the day....

At the other end of the "line" analogy, the court correctly identifies that "this book constitutes the archetypal example of speech which, because it methodically and comprehensively prepares and steels its audience to specific criminal conduct through exhaustively detailed instructions on the planning, commission, and concealment of criminal conduct, finds no preserve in the First Amendment."

Ideas(e)->——————A——————*——*Hit Man->* Overt Acts
Prepares and/or "steels"
an individual to commit murder

Placing *Hit Man* far towards the end of the "line" signifies that the book itself has such a close nexus to illegal activity that for First Amendment analysis it is more action than speech. It is the "extraordinary comprehensiveness, detail, and clarity" of the "how-to" murder that the book contains that negates any claim that it contains abstract advocacy of illegal activity.

For example, *Hit Man* goes into great detail about the different ways to dispose of the corpse, or "mark" after the "hit." It is clear that this type of minute detail in "how-to" perpetrate criminal activity is not the type of "speech" contemplated by the Court in *Brandenburg*, but, instead, is more akin to an "overt act" than an "idea."

> [In order to dispose of a corpse,] you can simply cut off the head after burying the body. Take the head to some deserted location, place a stick of dynamite in the mouth, and blow the telltale dentition to smithereens! After this, authorities can't use the victim's dental records to identify his remains. As the body decomposes, fingerprints will disappear and no real evidence will be left from which to make positive identification. You can even clip off the fingertips and bury them separately.

> [Or] you can always cut the body into sections and pack it into an ice chest for transport and disposal at various spots around the countryside.

> If you choose to sink the corpse, you must first make several deep stabs into the body's lungs (from just under the rib cage) and belly. This is necessary because gases released during decomposition will bloat these organs, causing the body to rise to the surface of the water.

> The corpse should be weighted with the standard concrete blocks, but it must be wrapped from head to toe with heavy chains as well, to keep the body from separating and floating in chunks to the surface. After the fishes and natural elements have done their work, the chain will drag the bones into the muddy sediment....

If you bury the body, again deep stab wounds should be made to allow the gases to escape. A bloating corpse will push the earth up as it swells. Pour in lime to prevent the horrible odor of decomposition, and lye to make that decomposition more rapid.

Suicide Solution–Ozzy Osbourne

Previously, I discussed the *McCollum v. CBS Records* case as an example where *Brandenburg*, and First Amendment doctrine generally, should not pose an absolute bar to a "shock tort" negligence cause of action filed against Ozzy Osbourne. The case is also illustrative in the context of the differing level of constitutional protection based on the "abstract" quality of the speech.

Here, it seems clear that the lyrics of the song "Suicide Solution" are remote ideas that do not contain the close nexus to "overt acts" to be criminalized under *Brandenburg*. The court categorized the lyrics as ideas akin to philosophical speech:

> Merely because art may evoke a mood of depression as it figuratively depicts the darker side of human nature does not mean that it constitutes a direct "incitement to imminent violence." The lyrics sung by Osbourne may well express a philosophical view that suicide is an acceptable alternative to a life that has become unendurable–an idea which, however unorthodox, has a long intellectual tradition.

The lyrics, if they are construed to be ideological or philosophical in nature, seem to be speech more similar to the "the mere abstract teaching…of the moral propriety or even moral necessity" of suicide and are thus protected under the First Amendment.

Ideas(e)-> [abstract advocacy]—-*—————A—————> Overt Acts
Does not prepare or
"steel" an individual to commit suicide

"How to Commit Suicide" Websites

Certain "pro-suicide" websites provide an excellent overview of the abstract line analysis as speech contained within a single website could fall on opposite ends of the "line."

Web content such as the *Practical Guide to Suicide* found online contains the type of specific instruction and promotion that might "steel" an individual to commit suicide. Thus, the content found in the following examples from the "Guide" would be found on the far right side of our line analysis almost melding into overt action.[201]

Under the title "Helpful Home Remedies," the "Guide" lists the following:

Shotgun to the Brainstem

Having a shotgun makes killing oneself a snap. Aim for the brainstem; be sure that there is a good foundation for the recoil before firing.

Potassium Cyanide (KCN) Consumption

If you've got some potassium cyanide, or know where you can get some, then the following method may prove valuable): [sic]

1. Take a small glass of cold tap water; do not use mineral water, nor any kind of juice or soda water, due to the acidity of such liquids.

2. Stir 1g (or 1.5g, at most) of potassium cyanide (KCN) into water; using more than recommended will likely cause burning of the throat due to the acidity.

3. After about five minutes–this "waiting period" is important, as a chemical reaction needs to take place–the KCN will be dissolved and ready to drink (because it turned into HCN). It remains drinkable for a period of several hours, but not much more than that.

4. Once the concoction is drunk, consciousness will be lost within a minute. There will just be time to rinse out the glass (to ensure no one else accidentally drinks from it–however, one could just as easily put a big "Warning" label onto the glass, or throw it into a corner or a fireplace, if one doesn't want to take the time) and lie down. But beware–a person extremely weakened by illness might lose consciousness within twenty seconds.

The "Guide" includes information on "Choosing a Method or Combination of Methods" to kill oneself. It includes information on poisons, (Ethylene Glycol (antifreeze)) cyanide, Potassium Chloride; depressants, ("LD-50"/"MLD–"minimum lethal dosage") alcohol, heroin and other controlled substances, barbiturates and sleeping pills; Carbon monoxide (CO) inhalation....unfortunately, this list goes on and on.

Ideas(e)->————————A———————[specific instruction]-*-> Overt Acts
Instructs, prepares and
"steels" an individual to commit suicide

On the other side of the figurative abstraction line is the content contained in websites that merely advocates a position that individuals should be able to choose death or that death is preferable to life. Certain items found on the Church of Euthanasia's website provides an examples of speech that is abstract in nature and does not prepare or "steel" an individual to suicide.[202] These items are not instructional or specific and do not actually assist, prepare or "steel" a person in committing suicide.

Ideas(e)-> [abstract advocacy]——*—————————A—————> Overt Acts
Does not prepare or
"steel" an individual to suicide

A Last Word:
After the Credits: NBK's Southern rampage of violence and death

> "The most pacifistic people in the world said they came out of this movie and wanted to kill somebody."
> Oliver Stone, director of *Natural Born Killers*

> "Life imitates art, according to the cliché, and, in some instances, so does death."[203]

On March 5, 1995, Sarah Edmonson and her boyfriend Ben Darrus, both eighteen, sat in a cabin in Tahlequah, Oklahoma, watching *Natural Born Killers* repeatedly and ingesting LSD tabs.

Early the next morning, the couple grabbed a .38 caliber revolver and hit the road. While cruising the highways, Darrus talked "crazy" about his desire to kill people just like "Mickey and Mallory" from *NBK*.

They headed south, although it isn't exactly clear where they were going. Inconsistent reports suggested that they had been heading to Florida to see the ocean, to New Orleans for *Mardis Gras* or to Memphis to see the Grateful Dead.

Wherever they were headed, on March 7, 1995, they happened upon a cotton gin near Hernando, Mississippi where Darrus walked in and shot Bill Savage, an elderly man and total stranger, twice in the head from point-blank range. After stealing some money Darrus fled, mocking Savage's dying groans as he drove.

The duo continued south down Interstate 55, towards Louisiana, and arrived the next evening around midnight at a Time Saver store in Ponchatoula, Louisiana. After being told that it was her turn now, Edmonson entered the store, shot the cashier, Patsy Byers and returned to the car. Realizing that she had forgotten to steal anything, Edmonson quickly returned to pilfer the cash register of the $105 it contained and while doing so said to the bleeding cashier, "Poor 'ol thing. You're not dead yet." Byers didn't die; she remains paralyzed below the neck.

Before rising to international fame as a novelist, John Grisham practiced law in DeSoto County, Mississippi. Grisham could frequently be found at the DeSoto County Courthouse and it was there that he first met Bill Savage.

After Savage's murder at the hands of Ben Darrus, Grisham wrote an article entitled, "Unnatural Killers" that was originally printed in the April 1996 issue of OXFORD AMERICAN magazine. In this article, Grisham addresses the causal link between movies such as *NBK* and the resulting "copycat" crimes associated with them.[204]

A case can be made that there exists a direct causal link between the movie *Natural Born Killers* and the death of Bill Savage. Viewed another way, the question should be: Would Ben have shot innocent people but for the movie? Nothing in his troubled past indicates violent propensities. But once he saw the movie, he fantasized about killing, and his fantasies finally drove them to their crimes.

The notion of holding filmmakers and studios legally responsible for their products has always been met with guffaws from the industry. But the laughing will soon stop. It will take only one large verdict against the likes of Oliver Stone, and his production company, and perhaps the screenwriter, and the studio itself, and then the party will be over. The verdict will come from the heartland, far away from Southern California, in some small courtroom with no cameras. A jury will finally say enough is enough; that the demons placed in Sarah Edmonson's mind were not solely of her making.

Once a precedent is set, the litigation will become contagious, and the money will be enormous. Hollywood will suddenly discover a desire to reign itself in.

The landscape of American jurisprudence is littered with the remains of large, powerful corporations which once thought themselves bulletproof and immune from responsibility for their actions. Sadly, Hollywood will have to be forced to shed some of its own blood before it learns to police itself.

Even sadder, the families of Bill Savage and Patsy Byers can only mourn and try to pick up the pieces, and wonder why such a wretched film was allowed to be made.[205]

John Grisham

Conclusion on the role of the First Amendment in private tort suits

In large part, the examination of the seemingly boundless interpretation that the First Amendment acts to bar lawsuits based on content-neutral tort principles between private individuals for money damages is an examination of the endless debate over rights vs. responsibilities in American culture and jurisprudence.

Over 50 years ago, Justice Reed, writing for the Court in *Kovacs v. Cooper*, stated "To enforce freedom of speech in disregard of the rights of others would be harsh and arbitrary in itself."[206] However, even if this extreme deference towards responsibility-free expression were to be desirable, this balance should not be created by the judiciary outside the express language of a ratified Amendment. Representative government should craft this balance through expression-related tort reform or other democratic means in a proactive instead of passive manner.

My argument, while seeking to reverse the breadth of the *New York Times v. Sullivan* contention, that whatever indirectly "chills" speech, regardless of the tenuous nature of governmental involvement (even in cases of private tort suits) invokes the First Amendment and is somehow the legally equivalent of the command that "Congress shall make no law…" is not so broad or revolutionary when looked at in a historical perspective.

Well over 200 years ago, when the First Amendment was no more than "a gleam in the eye of our founding fathers, if that…."[207] Sir William Blackstone stated:

Every free man has an undoubted right to lay what sentiments he pleases before the public; to forbid this is to destroy the freedom of the press; but if he publishes what is improper, mischievous, or illegal, he must take the consequences of his own temerity…. [208]

5

Religion and the First Amendment

The Pledge,
the Ten Commandments, and
"Walls" built out of bricks of populist interpretation

(A) *Tearin' Down the "Walls" of Populist Interpretation*

Amendment I [1791]

Congress shall make no law respecting an establishment of religion, or prohibiting the free exercise thereof...

Few areas of Constitutional interpretation have been affected as much by a popular perception as the first section of the First Amendment. The Amendment's proscription of governmental action to establish a religion and its simultaneous prohibition against taking action to interfere with an individual's right to exercise his respective religion puts this part of the Amendment in conflict with itself.

A letter written by Thomas Jefferson to a Baptist Association has muddied the waters even more and added to the resulting confusion about the Amendment's inner-conflict. Jefferson wrote the letter in response to an earlier letter from the Danbury Baptist Association asking him why he continued to refuse to proclaim national days of fasting and thanksgiving as Presidents Washington and Adams had done before him. The text of his letter, surely meant to appease the Baptists to some degree, has, over time, constructively been added as an Amendment to the simple language of the First Amendment:

71

"…I contemplate with sovereign reverence that act of the whole American people which declared that their legislature should make no law respecting an establishment of religion, or prohibiting the free exercise thereof, *thus building a wall of separation between church and state.*"
(in part) (emphasis added) (signed Thomas Jefferson January 1, 1802)

I ascribe to the general belief that this section of the First Amendment was meant to prohibit the federal government from "establish[ing]" a national religion similar to the Church of England that existed at the time of Constitutional writing and ratification.

Over time, this notion of a "wall of separation between church and state" has resulted in the belief that even the recognition of a supreme being, or any connection to "theism," must be completely stripped out of every aspect of public life. This reading is too broad.

Interestingly, it is Justice Black, who I cite to in previous contexts for his limited reading of the First Amendment, who takes the misguided step of reading Jefferson's broad language into the First Amendment. "The First Amendment," said Black, "has erected a wall between church and state. That wall must be kept high and impregnable. We could not approve the slightest breach."[209] The First Amendment doesn't erect anything. It is prohibited from establishing religion but this does not also mean that it is similarly and affirmatively required to "erect" this hypothetical "wall." While this "wall" may arguably be a positive addition to American governance, if it is to be erected at all, it should be through the efforts of representative government, not the interpretive arm of the federal courts.

Further, Jefferson's "wall" has become so main-stream that many individuals believe that it is necessary to derive the "original intent" or follow a "strict construction" view of Constitutional interpretation. For example, a recent article in a prominent national magazine began boldly, "I am a strict constructionalist and a firm believer in original intent."[210] The author goes on to state that due to these beliefs he feels the Pledge of Allegiance is "two words too long." Specifically, the words "under God," inserted into the Pledge in 1954 by Congress, violate America's sacred "wall of separation" and thus, the First Amendment.

The applicability of the First Amendment's "Establishment Clause" to the States through the Fourteenth Amendment is a somewhat curious development when viewed in light of the place of religion in Colonial America. There is little doubt that the Bill of Rights, generally, was written to address fears by the ratifying States that the central government would become too powerful. One primary area of concern was that the federal government would "establish" a central religion similar to the one found in England. It is not clear that there was any intention by the individual States to strip themselves of their power to establish a State religion. It is clear that the original intention of the Establishment Clause, to keep the federal government out of religion, has backfired and the federal government, through the federal courts, are more involved in shaping the boundaries and exercise of religion than ever before.[211]

(B)   The Pledge of Allegiance:

Given the present debate, no book related to the First Amendment would be complete without at least some reference to the controversy involving the Pledge of Allegiance. The U.S. Supreme Court has agreed to review the ruling of the Ninth Circuit and the final decision by the Court will take place after publication of this book.[212] Justice Scalia recused himself from taking part in the case, creating the possibility of a 4-4 deadlock which would affirm the Ninth Circuit Court of Appeal's ban on "under God."[213]

The background facts of the case leading to the national outrage at the Ninth Circuit's ruling that the words "under God" in the Pledge violate the Establishment Clause of the First Amendment are not only unremarkable, they are, in fact, drawn from classroom traditions of this Nation rooted in "Rockwellian" normalcy.

In following both California state law (Cal. Educ. Code § 52720 (1989)) (requiring that schools begin each day with "appropriate patriotic exercised") and school district policy that "[e]ach elementary school class [shall] recite the pledge of allegiance to the flag once each day," Michael Newdow's daughter, an elementary school student, was led by her teacher in the recitation of the following Pledge:

> *I pledge allegiance to the Flag of the United States of America, and to the Republic for which it stands, one nation **under God**, indivisible, with liberty and justice for all.*

The "under God" language was added to the original Pledge by Congress in 1954.

While the issue of whether a child could be compelled to recite the Pledge had been ruled on decisively by the U.S. Supreme Court in *West Virginia State Board of Education v. Barnette* in 1943, Newdow claimed that his daughter was injured when she was compelled to "watch and listen as her state-employed teacher in her state-run school leads her classmates in a ritual proclaiming that there is a God, and that our's [sic] is 'one nation under God.'"

There continues to be a great deal of controversy over whether Newdow's daughter was ever bothered (or injured) in the slightest by the daily recitation of the Pledge and whether Newdow had parental standing to file the suit on behalf of his daughter and whether he was truthful in pleadings filed with the courts.

It appears that Newdow's crusade has little to do with the welfare of his daughter, who lives with her mother and not Newdow, willingly recites the Pledge in school and attends a Calvary Chapel. Newdow, a physician who holds a law degree is not your run-of-the-mill *pro se* plaintiff and should be held accountable for any untrue claims made in the pleadings of this case.

Newdow said the following during a phone interview shortly after the Ninth Circuit's ruling in June 2002:

CNN: [question] At what point did your daughter come home to you and say she was ostracized for not saying the Pledge of Allegiance?

Newdow: [answer] My daughter is in the lawsuit because you need that for standing. I brought this case because I am an atheist and this offends me, and I have the right to bring up my daughter without God being imposed into her life by her schoolteachers. So she did not come and say she was ostracized.

It doesn't appear that Newdow is doing much to "bring up [his] daughter" with or without the influence of the public schools and the use of a child in this manner is highly questionable.

The usual reaction to news about the Ninth Circuit Court of Appeals, like the South Carolina Supreme Court, is "they did what?" On June 26, 2002 individuals throughout the nation furled a brow and asked in exasperation how a federal court could declare that the Pledge of Allegiance was unconstitutional.

Justice Goodwin, writing for the majority, summarized the quagmire that has become schoolhouse-Establishment Clause jurisprudence after a series of confusing cases that have each resulted in their own Constitutional "test."

> Over the last three decades, the Supreme Court has used three interrelated tests to analyze alleged violations of the Establishment Clause in the realm of public education: the three-prong test set forth in *Lemon v. Kurtzman*, 403 U.S. 602, 612-13 (1971); the "endorsement" test, first articulated by Justice O'Connor in her concurring opinion in *Lynch*, and later adopted by a majority of the Court in *County of Allegheny v. ACLU*, 492 U.S. 573 (1989); and the "coercion" test first used by the Court in *Lee*.

Goodwin expressly notes that "we [the court] are free to apply any or all of the three tests, and to invalidate any measure that fails any one of them." The Pledge then goes 0-3 according to the Ninth Circuit. ("…the policy and the Act fail the endorsement test."; Similarly, the policy and the Act fail the coercion test."; and "Similarly, the school district policy also fails the *Lemon* test.")

Judge Fernandez dissents as to the part of the Ninth Circuit's decision holding that the "under God" phrase violates the First Amendment. Fernandez, seemingly adopting the more restricted interpretation of the Establishment Clause, writes, "We should, instead, recognize that those clauses [Establishment; Free Exercise] were not designed to drive religious expression out of public thought; they were written to avoid discrimination." Fernandez goes on to conclude that:

> [L]egal world abstractions and ruminations aside, when all is said and done, the danger that "under God" in our Pledge of Allegiance will tend to bring is so miniscule as to be *de minimus*. The danger that phrase represents to our First Amendment freedoms is picayune at most.

The lesson, thus far, of Newdow's crusade to rid the Pledge of "under God" seems to be the danger of dicta. The Supreme Court has chosen to interpret the Constitution in a vague, sometimes intellectually dishonest, manner, erecting a confusing maze of balancing tests and fluid levels of scrutiny for Congress to muddle through, later allowing themselves the luxury of picking and choosing which test will either release slack or reign in laws that arise in the cases the Justices themselves choose to hear. But the trail of breadcrumbs is no more and this loosely formed world of "tests" and "scrutiny" can not only serve the Justices in achieving certain ends, but also allows lower courts to abstractly weave together a decision to say anything that can be said, armed with this endless array of tests, dicta, and wordy opinions (concurrences and dissents) written more, at times, to shape future law and policy than to decide the case between the two adverse litigants in the instant case.

First Amendment cases seem to provide the most colorful, and, at times, prophetic language, from Justice Jackson's "fixed star[s]" in "constitutional constellation[s]" in *West Virginia v. Barnette*[214] to Scalia's imagery of the flag only flying one way in Texas, the *Newdow* opinion is no exception. Although somewhat lengthy, Judge Fernandez's comments related to the potential reach of such a decision are worth repeating here:

> My reading of the stelliscript suggests that upon Newdow's theory of our Constitution, accepted by my colleagues today, we will soon find ourselves

prohibited from using our album of patriotic songs in many public settings. "God Bless America" and "America the Beautiful" will be gone for sure, and while the use of the first and second stanzas of the Star Spangled Banner will still be permissible, we will be precluded from straying into the third. And currency beware! Judges can accept those results if they limit themselves to elements and tests, while failing to look at the good sense and principles that animated those tests in the first place. But they do so at the price of removing a vestige of the awe we all must feel at the immenseness of the universe and our own small place within it, as well as the wonder we must feel at the good fortune of our country. That will cool the febrile nerves of a few at the cost of removing the healthy glow conferred upon many citizens when forbidden verses, or phrases, are uttered, read, or seen.

(C)   The Ten Commandments:
(a)   Has Congress acted?

The first question as to whether the act of placing the "Ten Commandments" monument in the rotunda of the Alabama State Judicial Building is whether "Congress" has acted to abridge speech? The district court opinion ordering Judge Moore to remove the monument states that the Constitution "provides that government shall make no law respecting an establishment of religion." How the First Amendment even applies in this matter is not clear. Judge Moore is not Congress and no law, of any kind, has been passed to "establish" religion.

In stating that "government 'shall make no law....'" the court holds that the First Amendment applies to the government generally even though the Amendment could not be clearer in its wording that "*Congress* shall make no law respecting an establishment of religion...."

(b)   The Controversy:

On July 31, 2001, Alabama Supreme Court Justice Roy Moore, without the knowledge or consent of his fellow Justices, had a 5,280-pound granite monument depicting the Ten Commandments placed in the rotunda area of the state judicial building in Montgomery, Alabama.

On August 1, 2001, in a speech given to present the new monument, Chief Justice Moore stated that he was "pleased to present this monument depicting the moral foundation of law."

Predictably, the U.S. District Court for the Middle District of Alabama held that the monument violated the Establishment Clause of the First Amendment.

The Eleventh Circuit affirmed the lower court's ruling on July 1, 2003 and ordered the monument removed from the state building.

Thou Shall Get Elected...

What makes this case somewhat different than the struggles to gain First Amendment protection for tattooing or Newdow's feud with two words of the Pledge, is the place of this Establishment Clause struggle in light of pragmatic and self-serving politics.

Chief Justice Roy Moore campaigns almost exclusively on the preservation of Judeo-Christian ideals as the foundation of secular law. A short history of Justice Moore is warranted. Moore began as a judge on the Circuit Court of Etowah County, Alabama. Soon after taking office, Moore "hung a hand-carved, wooden plaque depicting the Ten Commandments" behind his bench in the courtroom. He also routinely "invited clergy to lead prayer at jury organizing sessions." As a result of these actions, two high-profile lawsuits were filed against Moore in 1995. Both lawsuits were later dismissed on justiciability grounds. Following in the footsteps of cliché that no publicity is bad, especially in the "Bible-Belt" South, Moore made his tireless support of the Ten Commandments and the moral foundations of law the cornerstone of his campaign to become Chief Justice in November 2000. Throughout the campaign he was referred to openly as the "Ten Commandments Judge."

Similar to the figurative act of standing to block a University building's door upon the threat of integration, Judge Moore can be seen by a large number of constituents to be a protector of a return to traditional Christian morals at the same time protecting the sovereignty of a state, especially a Southern state, against an intrusive federal government.[215]

(c)   The aptly named "Lemon" test:

> "Like some ghoul in a late-night horror movie that repeatedly sits up in its grave and shuffles abroad, after being repeatedly killed and buried, *Lemon* stalks our Establishment Clause jurisprudence once again, frightening the little children and school attorneys of Center Moriches Union Free School District."[216]

Far removed from the text of the First Amendment which merely limits Congress from making laws that would respect "an establishment of religion" the precedent available to the U.S. District Court for the Middle District of Alabama, Northern Division, was the aptly named *Lemon* (of a) test.

The court, applying *Lemon*, stated "[f]or a practice to survive an Establishment Clause challenge, it 'must have a secular legislative purpose,…its principal or primary effect must be one that neither advances nor inhibits religion,…[and it] must not foster 'an excessive government entanglement with religion.'"[217] Similar to the fact that Chief Judge Moore is not "Congress" and he hasn't made any "law," the *Lemon*-test doesn't appear applicable because Judge Moore had no "legislative purpose" at all. Placing the monument in the rotunda, regardless of whether one thinks it is an appropriate place for it, isn't legislative action in any way; it isn't a piece of legislation.

Lemon effectively changes the Establishment Clause into the non-entanglement clause of the First Amendment. Similar to other areas of the First Amendment, we live under interpretive doctrine instead of within the "four corners" of the Constitution itself. If this Nation truly wants a "wall of separation" between church and state and a policy of strict non-entanglement that distances religion from every facet of public life, this is a question ripe to be decided by an Amendment to the Constitution, not decided by the most non-democratic body of our Republic. Similar to the drastic change imposed on the Constitution by the evolution of obscenity, I would agree with Justice Douglas in his sentiment that such revolutionary alteration of the First Amendment must only be "done by constitutional amendment after full debate by the people."

6

Judicial "Elitism" in America

Throughout this section of the book I will refer to what I call "judicial elitism" and a subset of "judicial elitism" I call "judicial paternalism." The two concepts are similar but not identical.

Judicial elitism is the tendency of the Supreme Court, and other courts, to afford different levels of protection to speech or expression based on the court's particular view of the speech or expressive activity in question. A subset of judicial elitism is judicial paternalism. Judicial paternalism is, generally, a court's view that it has to protect citizens from themselves.[218]

(A)   Strip Clubs and the First Amendment: G-Strings, Pasties, Judicial Elitism and the Naked Truth of Crumbling Federalism[219]

"The truth is all of us (to a greater or lesser extent) always want to step on those things we dislike. Perhaps that is natural. The problem is this "instinct" to use a misnomer is even greater and more frightening when it comes to the government. At its most basic level I think that is what the First Amendment is all about. It protects us from ourselves and reminds us why we live in such a cherished country. Without that type of barrier the government would run all over us. That is not very eloquent, but that must be why we all allow things to occur in our society that most of us find repugnant–Nazi's, the KKK, etc."[220]

While the entertainment afforded by a nude ballet at Lincoln Center to those who can pay the price may differ vastly in content (as viewed by judges) or in quality (as viewed by critics), it may not differ in substance from the dance viewed by the person who...wants some 'entertainment' with his beer or shot of rye.[221]

The line of cases involving strip clubs and their relationship with the First Amendment is a classic example of judicial elitism and the "culture wars" that

79

play out in the rulings of courts in many types of cases, including those involving the adult-entertainment industry.

Nudity has been part of live entertainment for centuries and continues in modern times. For instance, *Hair*, *Oh Calcutta!*, *Angels in America* and *The Grapes of Wrath* all include nudity as part of their live performance. Whether an individual is naked as part of a scene from *Gypsy*, or naked because some slob enjoys the wallet-draining tradition of paying to be teased, substantively, both are the same. There is someone (usually a female) naked in front of other people. As this is the case, what is really being criminalized, and in many cases left unprotected by the courts, is the message sent by one type of nudity and not another.

The initial fun part of reading, analyzing and digesting strip club cases is the opportunity to read the public indecency/indecent exposure statutes from which these cases stem.

For example, the Indiana statute that resulted in the 1991 U.S. Supreme Court case *Barnes v. Glen Theatre, Inc.* reads "[a] person who knowingly or intentionally, in a public place: (3) appears in a state of nudity has broken Indiana law. In this context, nudity is defined to include, "the showing of the covered male genitals in a discernibly turgid state." The general prohibition against criminalizing involuntary actions aside, it isn't clear in any way, how this law might be detected or enforced. Sad. A very entertaining line of cases from Seminole County, Florida's Public Decency Ordinance was related to a statute mandating that "[e]ach female person may determine which one-fourth of her breast surface area (see definition of breast) contiguous to and containing the areola is to be covered..." Even the judge in this case couldn't resist adding in a footnote:

> This exemption is apparently for the ladies of fashion who wear low cut dresses at cocktail parties both in Seminole County and in the City of Casselberry. They should remember that the exposure limit is 75% and no more. A caliper may be necessary in close cases.

The (*G?*) string of cases related to the First Amendment's effect on nude dancing is extensive. I have included here a number of significant cases that illustrate judicial elitism and the various legal doctrines that have been used to criminalize a message thought, by some, (or many) to be so low-brow, low-class and second-rate as to simply cease to exist.

Miller v. Civil City of South Bend

The facts in *Miller* are fairly simple: J.R.'s Kitty Kat Lounge, and the Glen Theatre, two strip joints, along with Darlene Miller and Gayle Sutro, two strippers, sued in federal court to enjoin the State of Indiana from enforcing its public indecency statute which proscribed nude and semi-nude barroom dancing.

After a significant amount of procedural history, the case was heard, *en banc*, by the Seventh Circuit Court of Appeals. The Seventh Circuit held that the indecency statute was unconstitutional and that it violated the First Amendment when used to prohibit "non-obscene expressive activity or public nudity."

What makes the *Miller* case entertaining, interesting, and relevant (especially in light of the fact that it was expressly overruled by the U.S. Supreme Court a year later) is the brilliant legal exchange by Judge Easterbrook and Judge Posner.[222]

The major issue between Posner and Easterbrook was whether erotic dancing is an "expressive activity" and thus deserving of First Amendment consideration. It seems that "expressive activity" would simply mean that a message it being conveyed, in any form by one person to another. Although by definition erotic dancing is expressive and communicative in nature, the court held the opposite: that a striptease dance is "mere conduct" and not "expressive activity."[223]

Posner clearly, and correctly, states that this conclusion, that erotic dancing is "mere conduct" is "indefensible and a threat to artistic freedom." Posner continued, detailing that it is the titillating nature of erotic dancing, and the fact that it creates a sexual longing in the viewer (the longing the next day for all that money you wasted) that makes erotic dance clearly expressive in nature.

> The goal of the striptease–a goal to which the dancing is indispensable–is to enforce the association: to make plain that the performer is not removing her clothes because she is about to take a bath or change into another set of clothes or undergo a medical examination; to insinuate that she is removing them because she is preparing for, thinking about, and desiring sex. The dance ends when the preparations are complete. The sequel is left to the viewer's imagination. This is the "tease" in "striptease."

Frank Easterbrook disagrees. His dissent is a good example of the type of "judicial elitism" that may contribute to differing levels of protection for what is substantively the same speech or conduct.

After pointing out that "[b]arroom displays are to ballet as white noise is to music," Easterbrook continues:

Sophisticates go to the museum and see Renoir's *Olympia* or to the opera and see a soprano strip during the Dance of the Seven Veils in Strauss' *Salome*. If the First Amendment protects these expressions, the argument goes, Joe Six-pack is entitled to see naked women gyrate in the pub. [internal citation omitted] Why does this follow? That a dance in *Solome* expresses something does not imply that a dance in JR's Kitty Kat Lounge expresses something, any more than the fact that Tolstoy's Anna Karenina was a stinging attack on the Russian social order implies that the scratching of an illiterate is likely to undermine the Tsar.

Continuing his dissent, Easterbrook follows this snobbish quote correctly stating that "The First Amendment does not let a government draw lines based on the viewpoint the performer expresses; it does inquire whether particular 'entertainment' is 'expression' in the first place. The Constitution does not protect 'the freedom of entertainment.'"

Next, Easterbrook confuses his analysis by apparently applying certain parts of the obscenity test created in *Miller*, (the other *Miller*) even though it is clear that the erotic dancing at issue is not obscene. If it were, it could be prohibited regardless of whether or not it was deemed expressive; the exception would apply. Easterbrook pulls the "taken as a whole, lacks serious literary, artistic, political or scientific value" prong of the *Miller*-obscenity test out of his hat and uses this to assert that "...the [Supreme] Court believes that the Constitution allows states to distinguish serious art from swill" and the fact that barroom dancing lacks "'serious...artistic...value' [this] assures us that Indiana is not squelching important aspects of culture."

Further, Easterbrook finds that "[s]tatutes may express moral views about how the community should live...[and]...[m]uch law is based on nothing than moral views." Easterbrook's easy acceptance of, and his failure to mention or address, the fact that this will be the morals of the majority, hence one of the primary reasons for the First Amendment is disturbing but telling. He avoids stating directly his belief that, not only does erotic dancing not have any cultural value, but it is immoral as well.

It seems that Easterbrook only detects expression when he, himself likes the message. His basic contempt for the tastes of "Joe Sixpack" is evident in one of his closing statements, "[m]aybe all of this is rationalization of a law that has no effects beyond depriving *hoi polloi* of a harmless pastime." Easterbrook's snooty dissent would be less frightening if hadn't been a sign of things to come.

Barnes v. Glen Theatre, Inc.

The *Narrowest* Tailoring: G-strings and Pasties

Unfortunately, *Barnes v. Glen Theatre, Inc.* was one of those "things to come." The Supreme Court's 1991, 5-4 plurality ruling in *Barnes* created what later proved to be a confusing and unworkable standard for lower courts, both state and federal, to apply.

The opinion, authored by Chief Justice Rehnquist and joined by Justices O'Connor and Kennedy, concluded that the First Amendment could apparently be divided geometrically in some fashion into perimeters. Rehnquist stated that "nude dancing of the kind sought to be performed here [at the Kitty Kat Lounge and Glen Theatre] is expressive conduct within the outer perimeters of the First Amendment, though we view it as only marginally so."[224] It would have been helpful if the Court had included a diagram of the different perimeters of the First Amendment.

Conceding, to whatever extent, that a First Amendment analysis was necessary, Rehnquist then turned to the four-part test for "speech-conduct" enumerated in *United States v. O'Brien*. The Court then works its way through *O'Brien*, making logical and not so logical leaps of faith to find that the Indiana statute at issue satisfied *O'Brien*.

The initial shortcomings of the Court's analysis are evident early on as Rehnquist must attempt to "balance" the suppression on expression and the "interests" of the State of Indiana despite the fact that "[i]t is impossible to discern, other than from the text of the statute, exactly what governmental interest the Indiana legislators had in mind when they enacted this statute, for Indiana does not record legislative history, and the State's highest court has not shed additional light on the statute's purpose."

Rehnquist's basic premise is that the challenged statute criminalizes nudity generally and does not target the expressive nature of exotic dancing. Even if we accept this as true, given the test set forth in *O'Brien*, the specific interests in question are to be balanced against the expression suppressed by even a neutral anti-nudity statute.

The Court, filling in the gaps for the fact that it isn't clear what Indiana's "important or substantial governmental interest" is, concludes that "[p]ublic indecency statutes such as the one before us reflect moral disapproval of people appearing in the nude among strangers in public places," and "the statute's purposes of protecting societal order and morality is clear…"

If we take at face value the fact that there is some traditional need to prohibit "people appearing in the nude among strangers in public places" this seemingly does not have anything to do with strip clubs. Are strip clubs really "in public?"

The Court's reasoning is circular and self-defeating. The Court takes solace in the fact that the expressive nudity within strip clubs can be banned because "[t]he appearance of people of all shapes, sizes and ages in the nude at a beach, for example, would convey little if any erotic message, yet the State still seeks to prevent it. Public nudity is the evil the State seeks to prevent, whether or not it is combined with expressive activity."[225]

Turned on its side, this statement is indicative of a poor ruling. The state of Indiana can ban nudity on beaches if it is true that it is not expressive conduct. The reason it can be banned is because it is not expressive; given the fact that the Court has earlier conceded that erotic dancing *is expressive*, it can not be banned in the same manner as pure conduct (such as the nude beach example) unless it can survive First Amendment scrutiny.

One aspect that the Court glosses over, in erroneously applying *O'Brien* to the Indiana anti-nudity statute, is that the statute in question is not truly a "general prohibition" on nudity...it is a "general prohibition" only on public nudity. The statute in *O'Brien*, criminalized the burning of a draft card, "at any time and in any place, even in completely private places such as the home." Clearly, this is not the case here...not even the State of Indiana has banned nudity inside the home.

So, returning to *O'Brien*, it is actually the State's interests in "societal order and morality" that are to be balanced against expressive conduct only to be viewed by consenting adults. As the dissent recognized:

> [t]he purpose of forbidding people to appear in nude in parks, beaches, hot dog stands, and like public places is to protect others from offense. But that could not possibly be the purpose of preventing nude dancing in theaters and barrooms since the viewers are exclusively consenting adults who pay money to see the dances. The purpose of the proscription in these contexts is to protect the viewers from what the State believes is the harmful message that nude dancing communicates.

The Court's plurality ruling falls into the same trap that the Supreme Court would later fall into with its shallow application of the "secondary effects" doctrine in *PAP's*: intellectual misdirection. The Court, in *Barnes*, states that "[l]ikewise, the requirement that the dancers don pasties and G-strings does not deprive the dance of whatever erotic message it conveys; it simply makes the message slightly less graphic." Here, the logic is that although the effect on the viewer between a completely nude dancer and a dancer wearing what the Court calls a "scant" amount of clothing (*i.e.* G-string and pastie) is only minimal or "slightly less graphic" nevertheless, the Court grants to this "scant" amount of clothing a high purpose when it comes to protecting "societal order and morality." The Court holds that the statute is "narrowly tailored" (the narrowest apparently) and that "Indiana's requirement that the dancers wear at least pasties and G-strings is modest, (again, Rehnquist missed the pun) and the bare minimum (missed again) necessary to achieve the State's purpose." Again, if you can follow this logically it means that a couple of ounces of material is "necessary" to protect the "societal order and morality" of the State of Indiana. The Court overestimates the need for G-strings and pasties for issues such as order and morality and underestimates the effect that G-strings and pasties have on the message that erotic dancing conveys.

Scalia concurs, agreeing that the judgment of the Court of Appeals must be reversed but on different grounds than the plurality. Scalia writes that the "challenged regulation must be upheld, not because it survives some lower level of First Amendment scrutiny, but because, as a general law regulating conduct and not specifically directed at expression, it is not subject to First Amendment scrutiny at all."

Scalia, following his well-known philosophy of "originalism" as he does in most cases, returned to the text of the Constitution, and held that, "[t]he First Amendment explicitly protects 'the freedom of speech [and] of the press'—oral and written speech—not 'expressive conduct.' When any law restricts speech, even for a purpose that has nothing to do with the suppression of communication…we insist that it meet the high, First-Amendment standard of justification." Scalia reasoned that this standard was only in effect for "speech" and not simply because a general regulation might restrict expression in a collateral fashion stating, "[i]t cannot reasonably be demanded, therefore, that every restriction of expression incidentally produced by a general law regulating conduct pass normal First Amendment scrutiny…"

Scalia continued, where the regulation "prohibits conduct precisely because of its communicative attributes, we hold the regulation unconstitutional." As such, I can give Scalia the benefit of the doubt on this argument the First Amendment is not implicated, in any manner, upon the facts in *Barnes*. I don't agree with this opinion, and neither over time has the Court, but, given Scalia's overall ideology, I can detect an honest appraisal of the case in his concurrence. As you will see, *below*, in my analysis of his position in *PAP's*, given the distinction of the Erie,

Pennsylvania law in question, I find his position unsupportable and untenable, and, as rarely is the case for Scalia, bordering on intellectually dishonest.[226]

City of Erie v. PAP's A.M.

Although *PAP's* is usually spoken of in the same breath, and the underlying facts of the two cases seen as synonymous, as *Barnes v. Glen Theatre, Inc.*, an important distinction exists between the laws under consideration by the U.S. Supreme Court in the two cases.

The Indiana Public Indecency/Indecent Exposure statute at issue in *Barnes* was facially neutral;[227] the Erie statute issue in *PAP's* was clearly not. In fact, the law passed by the Erie City Council following the Court's ruling in *Barnes* is a good example of how not to pass seemingly neutral legislation aimed to criminalize particular conduct.

The Preamble to the Erie anti-nudity ordinance states:

> WHEREAS, Council specifically wishes to adopt the concept of Public Indecency prohibited by the laws of the State of Indiana, which was approved by the U.S. Supreme Court in *Barnes v. Glen Theatre Inc., et al*, 501 U.S. 560, 111 S.Ct. 2456, 115 L.Ed.2d 504 (1991) for the purpose of limiting a recent increase in nude live entertainment within the City, which activity adversely impacts and threatens to impact the public health, safety and welfare by providing an atmosphere conducive to violence, sexual harassment, public intoxication, prostitution, the spread of sexually transmitted diseases and other deleterious effects.

Stating expressly that the law is aimed at "limiting…nude live entertainment within the City…" it is clear that this is not, in any way, a neutral ban on conduct, it is, on its face, a law aimed at "limiting" a type of expression that the U.S. Supreme Court has deemed to be worthy of First Amendment protections, even if it falls in the "outer ambit" of these protections.

The definition of "public place" in the Erie law also clearly demonstrates the intent:

> "Public Place" includes all outdoor places owned by or open to the general public, and all buildings and enclosed places owned by or open to the general public, including such places of entertainment, taverns, restaurants, clubs, theaters, dance halls, banquet halls, party rooms or halls limited to specific mem-

bers, restricted to adults or to patrons invited to attend, whether or not an admission is levied.

It seems that it would be difficult to find any place that people could gather in Erie, Pennsylvania that is not a "public place." "Indecency laws" and "anti-nudity" statutes were originally enacted so that "public places," *i.e.* places where you might find the general public (not the "general public" that chooses to go to strip clubs) would be free of such conduct where children and adults who didn't seek out such conduct could exist unaffected.

Yet, under Erie law, Kandyland, an establishment for adults seeking and consenting to view this type of entertainment, is, in fact, a public place.

The Supreme Court's ruling in *PAP's* is disturbing in several ways. First, the Supreme Court holding out the City of Erie's "important or substantial" governmental interest in deterring the "secondary effects" of all-nude dancing was sufficient to satisfy the test set forth in *O'Brien*. Next, the Court expanded the traditional scope of its "secondary effects" doctrine from one that justified zoning to one that would allow an outright ban of expression. Third, the Court showed its elitist cultural tendencies by incorrectly holding that any effect on nude dancing that resulted from the forced wearing of G-string and pasties was merely, *de minimus*. Lastly, the Court, perhaps because of a bruised ego, decided a case that was clearly moot and, in doing so, basically made a declaratory judgment outside of the Court's constitutional province.

Justice Stevens, in dissent, correctly identified that in *PAP's*, the Court "has now held that such [secondary] effects may justify the total suppression of protected speech" where the secondary effects doctrine had been previously limited to the "regulation of the location," or zoning, of "commercial enterprises." While the "secondary effects" doctrine may be valid in situations where "ample alternatives" exist and expressive activity is "zoned" to minimize these "secondary effects," in cases such as *PAP's*, where an outright ban on certain expressive activity will result, the result is a dramatic "chilling" of speech-expression.

In *Kingsley International Pictures Corporation v. Regents of the University of the State of New York*, Justice Stewart, writing for the Court, stated, "'Among free men, the deterrents ordinarily to be applied to prevent crime are education and punishment for violations of the law, not abridgment of the rights of free speech...'"[228] Certainly, there are numerous situations that have "secondary effects" that we, as a society, do not cower to and relinquish our First Amendment rights. For instance, there are "secondary effects" of protest rallies, picket lines, KKK meetings, political conventions, and numerous other types of activities at the core of the First Amendment.

We clearly do not stop detested groups such as the Ku Klux Klan from marching on the streets of America although there are numerous "secondary effects," some criminal, some not, that usually surround such an event. In 1999, the expected "secondary effects" of a Klan march cost the taxpayers of Defiance, Ohio, a small city of about 16,000 people, $17,500 (mostly in police overtime) for a one-hour Klan march. Given that there had been about two dozen Klan rallies during 1999, the overall cost to the small city was about $800,000. A single rally on August 21, 1999 in Cleveland, Ohio cost the city $537,000.

A common image in the newspapers and other media coverage of free-speech events such as KKK rallies, abortion clinics, the recent free-trade protests in the Pacific northwest, at furriers, and a countless other venues where Americans meet, greet and protest are police standing between two ideologically warring groups.[229]

But, free-speech can come to a halt if certain "secondary effects" exist outside of strip clubs? The burden should similarly fall on the government, and not the speaker, or speakers, (or dancers in this case) to protect the expressive rights of all involved. The Supreme Court has taken a valid zoning regulation, based on the concept of "ample alternatives," and never an outright ban, and used it to effectively "zone out" free speech in the context of erotic dancing.

The Court's consideration of the "secondary effects" doctrine since *Renton v. Playtime Theatres, Inc.,*[230] shows that the "secondary effects" doctrine was not meant to be applicable in situations where the statute at issue was related to the suppression of expression:

> Our "secondary effects" jurisprudence presupposes that the regulation at issue is *"unrelated to the suppression of free expression."*[231]

As such, "secondary effects" is clearly an incorrect doctrine to be applied in *PAP's* where the law expressly states that it is targeting a certain type (all-nude) dancing. ("…for the purpose of limiting a recent increase in nude live entertainment within the City")

Other recent cases illustrate the illogical, and highly suspect, nature of the Court's use of "secondary effects" to totally proscribe protected speech without any ample alternative.

In *Ashcroft v. Free Speech Coalition,*[232] the Court acknowledged, that the type of work at issue, sexually explicit images that appear to "depict minor children but were produced without using any real children" could promote illegal activity within the "subcultures of persons who harbor illicit desires for children and commit criminal acts to gratify the[se] impulses" and among the "serious offenders...who flirt with these impulses and trade pictures and written accounts of sexual activity with young children."

Nonetheless, although the *PAP's* Court held that a potential increase in criminal activity such as prostitution, car break-ins and the possibility of sagging property values were sufficient "secondary effects" to ban all-nude dancing, these "secondary effects" that might victimize children were not sufficient to ban "virtual" child pornography.[233]

For example, the Court stated, "Congress may pass valid laws to protect children from abuse...[t]he prospect of crime, however, by itself does not justify laws suppressing protected speech."[234] Couldn't it equally follow that, Congress may pass valid laws to criminalize prostitution and car break-ins, but, "[t]he prospect of crime, however, by itself does not justify laws suppressing protected speech[?]"[235]

Specifically to Congress' contention that virtual child pornography "whets the appetites of pedophiles...,"[236] what would appear to be of higher concern than prostitution or vandalism, the Court responds:

> The Government submits further that virtual child pornography whets the appetites of pedophiles and encourages them to engage in illegal conduct...[t]he mere tendency of speech to encourage unlawful acts *is not a sufficient reason for banning it.*[237]

Again, the employment of the "secondary effects" doctrine in *PAP's* is highly suspect. It is inherently tied to a pragmatic attempt by certain members of the Court to adjust the means to achieve calculated ends with a specific type of protected speech the Court seems to find "low-brow" and unsavory.

In the future, the "secondary effects" doctrine, if utilized in the future as it was in *PAP's*, to justify a complete ban of speech or speech-expression without any ample alternative, could be a drastic change of course in First Amendment jurisprudence.[238] "Secondary effects"[239] has, in the past, been primarily applied only to commercial enterprises, namely adult entertainment businesses. The most likely defense to the use of "secondary effects" in *PAP's* is that "the governmental interest in combating [secondary effects] is not at all inherently related to expression,"[240] but this distinction does nothing to remedy the use of "secondary effects" to justify an outright ban on speech-conduct the Court finds unsavory.

Yet, at the same time it acknowledges that the "potential" for crime (and other secondary effects) should not render protected speech defenseless from proscription.[241]

As previously stated, the *PAP's* ruling is disturbing in many ways. Most disturbing of all may be its simple logical fallacy. In sum, the Court holds that G-strings and pasties won't have any substantial effect on the expressive quality of the erotic dancing going on *inside* the club. In other words, the difference in the viewing experience for those watching it between a naked dancer and one wearing a G-string and pasty will only be "de minimus."

However, if the dancers wear what amounts to a spaghetti strap between their legs and small dots over their nipples, this will have some substantial effect on the crime and "secondary effects" happening *outside* the club. Naked women: property values plunge, cars are broken into and prostitutes come out in hoards. Women wearing G-strings and pasties: property values regain their strength, cars are spared, and the prostitutes flee like roaches in the light. This doesn't pass the laugh test.[242]

Peek-A-Boo Lounge

The continued dilemma of *Erogenous Zoning*

In *Peek-A-Boo Lounge of Bradenton, Inc. v. Manatee County, Florida*,[243] the Eleventh Circuit Court of Appeals exhaustively reviewed the line of cases involving both zoning and nudity bans related to strip clubs.

On November 24, 1998, the Manatee County Board of County Commissioners enacted an ordinance which amended its existing "Adult Entertainment Code" (part of the Manatee County Code of Laws) to provide specific physical requirements for adult dancing establishments.[244] Four months later, the county adopted "Public Nudity Ordinance 99-18" which made it unlawful to "knowingly, intentionally, or recklessly appear, or cause another Person to appear, Nude in a Public Place."[245] Although the ordinance was not directed at adult entertainment establishments on its face, the stated aim of the ordinance was, *inter alia*, to prevent:

> "[I]ncidents of prostitution, sexual assaults and batteries [and] other criminal activity" that the County found to be associated with the "mere appearance of nude persons in public places." The ordinance identified "public places" to include "streets, sidewalks, parks, beaches, [and] businesses and commercial establishments." Ordinance 99-18 also defined "nudity" broadly, to include,

the wearing of any opaque swimsuit or lingerie covering less than one-third of the buttocks or one-fourth of the female breast. Further, the ordinance specifically prohibited erotic dancers and others from appearing in public places wearing "G-strings, T-backs, dental floss, and thongs."[246]

Manatee Ordinance 99-18 attempts to expand the *PAP's* ruling and, as the Eleventh Circuit correctly indicates, attempts also to "redraw[n] the boundary between nudity and non-nudity, thereby prohibiting erotic dancers from wearing the amount of body covering the Court found to be consistent with the First Amendment in *PAP's*...."

The Eleventh Circuit held that since erotic dancers were prohibited from performing in the G-string and pasties, as provided for in *PAP's*, that Ordinance 99-18 could significantly impact the erotic message and therefore failed under the fourth prong of *O'Brien*.

While it is somewhat comforting to know that the faulty logic which underlies the *PAP's* ruling was not allowed to expand to require, under the *de minimus* guise, more than a G-string and pasties, a separate part of the opinion reveals continuing damage created by the *PAP's* precedent. In evaluating 99-18, the Circuit Court correctly identifies that:

> The Supreme Court has held that this type of governmental regulation which does not "target nudity that contains an erotic message," but rather "bans all public nudity regardless of whether that nudity is accompanied by expressive activity," is content-neutral and thus "should be evaluated under the framework set forth in *O'Brien*." *Pap's A.M.*, 529 U.S. at 289-90.[247]

It is unclear why Ordinance 99-18 is seen as a ban on all public nudity. Specifically, in the Preamble to the Ordinance, the County states that "there may be instances where appearing Nude in a Public Place may be expressive conduct incidental to and a necessary part of the freedom of expression that is protected by the United States or Florida constitutional provisions."

How can this possibly be a "ban [on] all public nudity regardless of whether that nudity is accompanied by expressive activity," when it appears that there is an express "savings clause" in the law to allow for certain, unnamed types of public nudity *if the nudity is* accompanied by expressive conduct?

This "content-neutral" Ordinance also has an exemption for any "bona fide live communication, demonstration, or performance...[that] is not a guise or pretense utilized to exploit nudity for profit or commercial gain." In other words, the Ordinance is content-neutral in relation to all-nudity, unless this nudity is deemed to be "bona fide" in nature. This culturally elite language is common in so-called "content-neutral" anti-nudity laws. Since the nudity in *Hair* and the nudity at the Peek-A-Boo lounge are both used for "profit or commercial gain"[248] it is unclear as to who decides what types of nudity are or are not a "guise or pretense utilized to exploit nudity." These types of legislatively-created, yet fluid, cultural and moral standards are easily utilized to oppress expressive content based on its "perceived quality" and many times "unpopular" or "lowbrow" appeal.

Club Juana

Elitism is not solely the territory of the judiciary. In many cases, legislatures get in on the act as well. Seminole County, Florida passed its Public Decency Ordinance in an attempt to outlaw nude and semi-nude dancing. The ordinance does not outlaw all nudity, in fact it doesn't even outlaw all public nude-dancing. The ordinance draws a distinction between dancing that is done as a "mere guise or pretense utilized to exploit the conduct of being nude for profit or commercial gain…" and nudity and nude (or semi-nude) dancing that "…constitutes a part of a *bona fide* live communication, demonstration or performance by a person…"

As most of these "*bona fide* live communication[s]" and "performance[s]" are going to require a ticket, it appears that even this "*bona fide*…communication" is going to be "for profit or commercial gain." Regardless, the language of this ordinance is clear that as long as the performance or communication involves a message seen, by the court or the police apparently, as "bona fide" it is allowed, otherwise one is "exploit[ing] the conduct of being nude…."

This exception serves to provide the ordinance with an obvious achilles' heel that was ripe to be "exploited" or tested by an energetic bunch of First Amendment purists down in suburban Orlando, Florida.

In an effort to protest this elitist and unfair law, the management of Club Juana contacted playwright and journalist Morris Sullivan and hired him to develop a theatrical program for a trio of exotic dancers to be performed at the club. The end result was several original interpretations of classic theater. The resulting work *Femmes Fatale* included the witches scene from Shakespeare's *Macbeth*, an adopted S&M scene from the *Marquis de Sade*, a scripted parody of the Sam Spade detective novels and even some cyber-sex fantasy thrown in for good measure.

On May 28, 1999, the play, *Femmes Fatale* opened in Casselberry, Florida and lasted about 40 minutes. A "review" as it were, in a Court TV article is too good to pass up:

> Maggie Morgan debuted as a Shakespearean actress in conditions that were less than ideal. She performed naked. The "theater" was a strip club. The sound system was broken, the lighting was dim and everyone in the audience who wasn't a cop, a reporter, or a lawyer was drunk. To cap it all, a critic labeled her interpretation of a witch in Macbeth as "wooden."

Ms. Morgan, an exotic dancer and First Amendment activist, spoke about her performance and the importance of the production, "[t]he law needs to be changed, and if this is what it took to change it—me naked stirring a cauldron—then so be it."

The vice cops (likely after watching the show in its entirety) charged the dancers/actresses with violation of Casselberry's nudity ban. The deep pockets of the adult-entertainment industry got involved and the cases headed for the courts. The case made its way to The Circuit Court of the Eighteenth Judicial Circuit, Seminole County, Florida and two opinions written in relation to the case by Judge O.H. Eaton, Jr. are staunch examples of First Amendment triumph.

In December 1999, the court ruled on an "Amended Order Denying Temporary Injunction." In this decision, Judge Eaton denied a temporary injunction sought by Plaintiffs that they did not have to don g-strings and pasties as required, but also held that the performance of *Femmes Fatales* fit within the "bona fide" performance exception as it contained "political parody and satire—elements which are in the best of American traditions." The Judge, in an entertaining opinion, joking in footnotes that the time of the performance wasn't exactly known because one of the dancers wasn't wearing a watch (or much else apparently) and that the court would not "divulge how many times" it had watched the tape of the performance which was made part of the record, further held that though *Femmes Fatales* was not near "Broadway quality" the performance was more "entertainment for adults" and not "adult entertainment."

Naked Truths of Nude Dancing

It seems there can be nothing more dangerous than the Supreme Court, or any court, making determination on what is, in effect, "essential."[249] In *Barnes*, and again in *PAP's*, the Court takes it upon itself to judge how important or essential total nudity is to dancing that they have conceded is "expressive." The Court holds that the viewer isn't "deprive[d]...of whatever erotic message it conveys" when the dancers don G-strings and pasties instead of being nude, it is simply less "graphic." (What if "graphic" was the message?)

Because the Court doesn't hold in any esteem, or place any value on "whatever erotic message it conveys," it sees no harm in detracting from what it already finds to be a message of minimal value. There can be a no more dangerous "slippery slope" for expressive freedoms than when courts unilaterally decide at what point an audience is "deprived" of a "message."[250]

The unfettered willingness of the Court to engage in intellectually dishonest evaluations of reality to impose its own type of elitist "ratings" on what does and does not deserve protection is truly disturbing.

Strip clubs are about sex, or, more accurately, paying to be teased. A bunch of drunk men ogle what are usually a bevy of cosmetically enhanced (and often chemically induced) young women who have mastered that public-speaking tactic of finding a spot above the audience's head and staring at it (...yeah, she's looking right in your eyes cowboy) all the while attempting to navigate the pole, shade her eyes from the glare of the rotating disco ball and siphon the maximum amount of money out of the crowd in a *quid pro quo* exchange for flesh before the end of the song.

As such, the societal value of strip clubs is likely marginal at best. However, it seems clear that a court's willingness to simply dismiss the act of a woman seductively taking off her clothes as having no expressive quality to those who view it is simply unrealistic and indicative of a higher hypocrisy that pervades certain First Amendment cases.

(B)   Tattoos on Trial
Author's Note:
White v. South Carolina

Writing the *amicus brief* in *White v. South Carolina*, Ron White's struggle to claim First Amendment protections for the art of tattooing, was incredibly fun. Ron, a burly 6'4" tattoo artist from Florence, South Carolina, was truly fighting the good fight, and he became a friend. Of the dozens of phone calls I traded with Ron in the months we worked together, I would say only a handful were before 2 a.m. (my time in Memphis), after 3 on the east coast where Ron was living.

My part in the case was as co-author of an *amicus brief* to submit to the United States Supreme Court on behalf of the National Tattoo Association and the Alliance of Professional Tattooists. What made the task even more satisfying was that it gave me the opportunity to work with Professor George Cochran, my Constitutional Law professor during law school, and someone who had been, and continues to be, a mentor and friend.

Kenneth Starr, former judge and independent counsel who became a household name during the Monica Lewinski scandal involving then-President Clinton, joined on with his firm KIRKLAND & ELLIS to represent Ron *pro bono* (free). Working closely with Ken was another very talented attorney, Ryan Phair, also a member of the D.C. office of KIRKLAND & ELLIS.

In conducting the research for the brief, I had the pleasure of meeting the very talented artists and piercers at Southern Draw Skin Art Studio in Sevierville, Tennessee. PLAYBOY picked up on the case and highlighted it in the magazine's "*Forum*" column.[251] The good folks at PLAYBOY were nice enough to publish a follow-up letter I wrote to clarify some of the issues in a subsequent issue. I even received an encouraging e-mail from Jesse James, West Coast Choppers legend and tattoo aficionado.

I was disappointed when the U.S. Supreme Court denied *certiorari* and declined to hear the case. Given the tiny fraction of cases the Court chooses to hear each term we expected this, but we held out hope until the end. The following chapter details why I felt that this was an important case and still is an important topic.[252]

White v. South Carolina–An Overview

On March 4, 2002, the South Carolina Supreme Court banned and criminalized an entire art form. The court held that the "act of tattooing falls on the unprotected side of the [First Amendment] line."[253] The court held that since there may be inherent risks to the art of tattooing, this fact alone exempted the regulation from all First Amendment scrutiny. If such health risks do actually exist, and this was never clear from the record before the court, this should merely lead to the proper balancing between these risks and the interests of the state under proper First Amendment analysis.

The South Carolina Supreme Court's ruling is rife with judicial elitism, paternalism, intellectual dishonesty and threats to artistic freedom. This section focuses on what I view as possibly the most subtle, yet direct threat: separating the collective processes that result in the creation of art, and viewing each individually under the laws of speech-conduct and the test set forth under *O'Brien*.

The facts of the case are simple and straightforward. Ron White, in an act of civil disobedience, went on television and violated a South Carolina criminal statute which prohibited tattooing. Although the facts of the case remain clear, the following section illustrates a subtle, yet dangerous, doctrinal outcome of the case.

Art is not the Constitutional Sum of its "Conduct"ive Parts

Acts of "completed" speech-conduct such as burning a flag or burning a draft card are protected under the First Amendment if they are "sufficiently communicative in character."[254] Determining this "character" and the sufficiency of its communicative nature, the Supreme Court has asked (1) whether an intent to convey a particularized message was present; and (2) whether the likelihood was great that the message would be understood by those who viewed it."

This communicative nature may be applicable to speech-conduct such as burning a draft card or a flag because, if people watching don't know it is a draft card you are littering; if they don't know you are burning a flag it is just arson. In these examples, the "completed" act of the speech-conduct can be evaluated under the principles set forth in *O'Brien*.

Applying *O'Brien*, and its progeny, to art, and dissecting the processes that lead to finished art and evaluating them individually as conduct, is scary within the context of artistic freedom. Obviously, if the steps and processes that lead to art can be criminalized individually, the artwork, and indirectly the content of that artwork, can be effectively "chilled." The state supreme court asserted that "[White] has not made any showing that the *process* of tattooing is communicative enough to automatically fall within First Amendment protection." In a simplistic manner, the court seemed to be considering this "protection" in its absolute form. In other words, if tattooing was protected by the First Amendment it meant that the state was powerless to address any perceived threats to health and safety.

"Protected" by the First Amendment, in this context, would only mean that the state would have to set forth these health risks and then they would be balanced, consistent with First Amendment jurisprudence, with the expressive freedoms of the artist. Instead, the court held that an entire, ancient art form was not worthy of *any* consideration under the First Amendment.

If the conduct which comprises the processes in the creation of art can be criminalized and the regulations criminalizing them given low scrutiny review by courts, the fallout could be drastic. For example, a state could pass a regulation banning sculpture because a sculptor could chip off a piece of rock or marble and injure his eye. If a court gave this regulation low scrutiny review and denied the *process* of sculpting any protection under the First Amendment, then the process of sculpting could be criminalized. Obviously, although the finished work may be protected regardless of content, there would still be a chilling effect on an entire art form in a given jurisdiction. Similarly, a state could pass a regulation banning the use of rappelling or scaffolding to paint murals. There are inherent risks to each of these "processes" if the artist were to fall. If a court gave the same low scrutiny review to the conduct that leads to finished artwork as the South Carolina Supreme Court did, the murals themselves would be protected, yet creating them would be next to impossible. If low scrutiny review was the standard to evaluate the constitutional protections for each process or step necessary to create art, the opportunity for state proscription is almost endless. There are some inherent risks to almost any type of art. For instance, dancers and actors can be injured, artists use blowtorches to weld metal together to create sculpture, and mimes get beat up on a regular basis.[255]

(C)   Good Clean, Nasty, Fun...Banned in the U.S.A.

"[T]he taste of any public is not to be treated with contempt. It is an ultimate fact for the moment, whatever may be our hopes for a change."[256]

Another example of judicial elitism, and especially the elitist nature of the application of the *Miller*-test, came in the early 1990's in the high-profile case involving the rap-music group 2 Live Crew. In 1989 2 Live Crew released the recording *As Nasty As They Wanna Be.* ("*Nasty*") By mid-February 1990, the Broward County Sheriff's office had received complaints about the recording and began an investigation.

On February 26, 1990, a Broward County Sheriff's deputy visited a retail music store and purchased a cassette version of *As Nasty As They Wanna Be.* The deputy listened to the cassette, had six of the album's eighteen songs transcribed and prepared an affidavit for the Broward County Circuit Court requesting that the court find probable cause that the album was obscene. After reviewing the album "in its entirety[,]" Judge Grossman explicitly found probable cause that the recording was obscene in violation of Florida Statute § 847.011. After receiving and making copies of the Judge's Order, the Broward County Sheriff's

Department provided retail merchants throughout the county with notice, through various means, that selling the *Nasty* album was a crime.

2 Live Crew, through their management company, filed an action in federal court to dispute the *Nasty*-ban. In June 1990, the Federal Court in the Southern District of Florida released its opinion in *Skyywalker Records, Inc. v. Navarro*[257] ruling that, as a matter of law, the *Nasty* recording was obscene and therefore was unprotected by the First Amendment.

Judge Gonzalez welcomed the task of making omnipotent determinations of fact, based, it appears, solely on his opinions and perceptions of what is and what should be. He begins an elitist opinion in somewhat patronizing fashion: "[t]his is a case between two ancient enemies. Anything Goes and Enough Already."[258] "Enough" of what "Already" is never clearly answered, but Gonzalez makes up for it by giving an opinion so thoroughly detailed to make the reader almost forget what becomes painfully clear as the opinion goes on. When all is said and done, the sum total of the *Skyywalker Records* opinion is one man with a life term deciding what falls just inside, or just outside, the protections of the First Amendment.[259]

Gonzalez's opinion is front-loaded in such a way that it boldly proclaims that because the obscenity exception exists within the framework of First Amendment jurisprudence, and because Florida has chosen to enact a state law against obscenity, that the determination of whether *Nasty* itself is obscene is some kind of forgone conclusion that should exist without review or criticism. Gonzalez then attempts a type of "divide and conquer" strategy to again confuse the issue as to whether *Nasty* is obscene by asserting that the only way that *Nasty* is not obscene is if obscenity ceases to exist as an exception to the First Amendment.

> An argument underlying the plaintiffs' position is that the obscenity or non-obscenity of any material should not be a concern of the criminal law, but rather should be left to the free market of ideas. Let each individual member of the public decide whether they wish to buy the material. 2 Live Crew has labeled their work with an explicit warning. They claim this label allows adults who would object to the recording's contents to exercise the consumer's free choice to not buy the product. To use the example of television, if the viewer does not like what he sees on Channel X, he may switch to Channel Y or turn off the set. In the case of obscene music, people who do not want to listen to obscenity do not have to buy it.
>
> This is the argument of those absolutists who believe *all speech, regardless of its content*, is protected by the First Amendment. Such individuals label all regulation of speech as "censorship" and "paternalism". This absolutist view finds

strength among those who believe rugged individualism is a valued virtue, if not a protected right that everyone should be permitted to "do their own thing."

This is a facially appealing argument. The problem is that it is not the law.

...

The absolutists and other members of the party of Anything Goes should address their petitions to the Florida Legislature, not to this court. If they are sincere let them say what they actually mean–Let's Legalize Obscenity![260]

To be critical of the court's opinion in *Skyywalker Records*, that *Nasty* is obscene, does not necessarily equate to either the belief that the obscenity doctrine should be abolished or that "...*all speech, regardless of its content*, is protected by the First Amendment."[261] It is not clear whether someone critical of Gonzalez's unilateral determination about this particular recording would believe that all speech, including, say, bomb threats, must be protected by the First Amendment as a member of the "Anything Goes"[262] party.

A determination under *Miller* that *Nasty* is not obscene is not the same thing, necessarily, as the belief that *all* obscenity must be legalized. But, Gonzalez remains on the defensive later in his opinion similarly stating:

In sum, if persons subscribe to the view that obscenity should be legalized, they should take their petitions to Tallahassee, the Florida capital, not to the steps of the U.S. Courthouse.[263]

The Judge entirely forgets that the actual Plaintiffs in this case only came to the "steps of the U.S. Courthouse"[264] because that is where the maze of procedural confusion that is obscenity law under *Miller* sent them. Due to ambiguous and *post facto* nature of the *Miller*-obscenity determination, only after releasing their art into the stream of commerce were the plaintiffs put on any type of notice that there work was, in fact, legally obscene. Judge Gonzalez, now being elitist, patronizing and paternalistic, lectures the citizenry that "[i]t is much easier to criticize the law, however, than it is to work to repeal it."[265]

Gonzalez apparently wishes to distance himself from the weight of his unilateral determination stating that "this court's role is merely to interpret the law to determine whether the particular material is obscene."[266] In this instance, Gonzalez appears to be either overlooking, or wishing to overlook, that, given the absence of a jury in this matter, the "mere" interpretation of law in this matter is the sole authority to determine whether the work receives protection under the First Amendment.

The utilitarian failings of *Miller* first become apparent with regards to Judge Gonzalez's determination as to the "relevant community." The Judge states, "Both parties [a]pparently [sic] assumed that the relevant community was only Broward County, Florida." The Judge disagrees with the parties on this point and asserts that "...the boundaries of the relevant community under *Miller* are a matter for judicial, not legislative, determination."[267] The Judge then determines that the "relevant community[,]" a major factor in the outcome of whether *Nasty* is going to be found obscene is not just Broward County, Florida, but also "Palm Beach, Broward, and Dade Counties."[268] Under *Miller*, it appears the Judge is on his own in making this determination, proceeding, without any guidance, through a litany of factors he finds relevant to form the outer boundaries of the First Amendment in a breezy and freestyle manner.[269]

The court then moves on to determine the "compositions of the citizens of this area."[270] Given that the court has gone to great lengths in the preceding paragraphs of the opinion to detail the "distinct mix of ethnic peoples" and generally allege its diversity, as well as the "tourist[y]" nature of the three counties, this task seems daunting, intellectually dishonest and not worthy of its place in the determination of fundamental civil rights such as freedom of speech and press, and illogical when viewed inside the mind of a single person.[271]

The void between a workable standard and the potential for vast abuses in judicial elitism becomes more apparent with the statement, "[t]he court, as the finder of fact, must rely upon its own personal knowledge...[in determining the 'composition of the citizens']...'of this area.'"[272] Then again, the tragedy of this type of singular analysis becomes apparent when the court concludes that the very nature of the community itself makes it that much harder to be classified or understood for the purposes of "the community standard's doctrine" under *Miller*:

> In a word, this area is remarkable for its *diversity*. The three counties...(not two or four—just because the court says so)...are a mecca for both the very young and the very old. Because of the beachs [sic] and the moderate year-round climate, this area includes young persons establishing homes and older residents retiring to enjoy life under the sun. There are both families and single individuals residing in the communities. Generally, the counties are *heterogeneous* in terms of religion, class, race, and gender.[273]

Under *Miller*, a single judge will define the boundaries of what does and does not fall under the sacred protections of the First Amendment after unilaterally determining that three counties make up the "relevant community[,]" and then determining that the defining characteristics that comprise the "composition of the citizens" that one can then derive "community standards" from are "diversity" and "heterogeneous."[274] In other words, the court is able to determine the "standards" of a community with made up boundaries, from "its own personal knowledge" about the community even though the defining characteristics of the community (from the court's determination) are that it is diverse and heterogeneous in the areas of "religion, class, race and gender."[275]

The most susceptible part of the *Miller*-test to judicial elitism is the "Social Value" prong. The court correctly recognizes that the third part of the *Miller*-test, whether the "*Nasty* recording, taken as a whole, lacks serious literary, artistic, political or scientific value" is not measured by community standards but, is, instead, measured by a "reasonable person" standard.[276] The court is aware of the potential criticism to a single judge interpreting the "value" of art. The opinion expressly states that neither "Rap" or "Hip-Hop" are on trial, that it was not the role of the court to act as censor or critic and that "[i]f the Nasty recording has serious literary, artistic, political, or scientific value, it is irrelevant that the work is not stylish, tasteful, or even popular."[277]

The court believes that the "…key to judging the *Nasty* recording is to consider it as a whole."[278] After noting the extreme difficulty in deeming music to be obscene, ("Initially, it would appear very difficult to find a musical work obscene…as noted by the [ACLU] the meaning of music is subjective and subject only to the limits of the listener's imagination."[279]) the court pragmatically deconstructs the *Nasty* recordings to find a way.

The court states:

> Taking the work in its entirety, the several riffs do not lift *Nasty* to the level of a serious artistic work. Once the riffs are removed, all that remains is the rhythm and the explicit sexual lyrics which are utterly without any redeeming social value.[280]

The court attempts to view a "work in its entirety" by taking it apart. How can the Judge possibly take "…the work in its entirety" if he is removing the riffs and judging just a part of the work which he then determines is "utterly without any redeeming social value."

7

The First Amendment and the F-word

On July 1, 2003 at 3:07 pm, Deputy State Public Defender Eric Vanatta filed a Motion with the District Court of Larimer County, Colorado. The "*Motion to Dismiss: The Constitutionality of Fuck, "Fucker" and "Fucking Fag"* made the national press and was too good for me to pass up here.

The trouble started when a student called his principal a "fucker, a fag, and a fucking fag" after being confronted by the principal about smoking in the boy's room. The student was charged with "*Interference with Staff, Faculty or Students of Educational Institutions*" which is a misdemeanor in Colorado.[281] The student was also suspended from school. Although Vanatta agreed that the student's suspension was "an entirely legal and appropriate reaction to the alleged statements," he argued that the criminal charge violated the student's rights under the First Amendment.[282] I had the opportunity to talk with Eric about the case–I appreciate him taking the time.

Anyone who has even a remote interest in the First Amendment should read the text of the Motion:

MOTION TO DISMISS: THE CONSTITUTIONALITY OF FUCK, "FUCKER" AND "FUCKING FAG"

Counsel hereby asks the Court to dismiss the case at bar. He states the following:

1. Mr [] is charged with interference with Staff, Faculty or Students of Educational Institutions, a class three misdemeanor. The charge was amended from the original charge of disorderly conduct.

2. The basis of the prosecution is an alleged statement Mr. [] made to his principal at school. During lunch, Mr. [] was contacted by the vice principal for

suspicion of smoking in the boy's room. He was taken to the principal's office where he allegedly called the principal a "fucker, a fag and a fucking fag." He was charged with the present offense based on his statements to the principal and he is being prosecuted for the words he spoke.

3. In order to provide a context for the alleged crime, we must first examine the history of Fuck and its evolution in society. Fuck's earliest recorded use is prior to the year 1500 from the English-Latin poem Flen Flyys: "Non sunt in celi quia fuccant uujuys of heli," which translates to "they are not in heaven because they fuck the wives of Ely." See www.wikpedia.org/wiki/fuck.

4. Although still offensive to some, Fuck is a more commonly used and accepted term in today's twenty-first century society than it was in the past. Use of the word Fuck "has been accepted in R-rated movies (and occasionally PG-13 movies, though not so often). Since the 1970's, the use of the word Fuck in R-rated movies has become so commonplace in mainstream American movies that it is rarely noticed by most audiences." *Id.* Some movies such as Scarface, Porky's and Goodfellas are known for the extensive use of the family of Fuck words (Fuck, Fucking, Fucker, Fuckface, Fucked, Absofuckinglutely, etc.) and in the non-US version of the comedy Four Weddings and a Funeral, Fuck is the chief word and repeatedly uttered during the first five minutes of the film. *Id.* Pulp Fiction was nominated for seven academy awards and took home the Oscar for *best screenplay* with its zealous and gratuitous use of Fuck phrases. It would be farfetched to argue that the Fuck family has not made its way into mainstream society.

5. In the world of the performing arts, Fuck and its many variants are not limited to Hollywood and the big screen. George Carlin, a well known and admired American comedian, for years has based his act on the use of the more colorful words in the English language, including extraordinary large amounts of Fuck phraseology. In fact, one of the most well known comedic skits in American history is George Carlin's "Seven Dirty Words," two of which are Fuck and Motherfucker. Andrew Dice Clay, Eddie Murphy, Chris Rock, Robin Williams and countless others have used the Fuck family to entertain audiences across the land, enriching their lives with the entertainment and comedic value of Fuck and its progeny.

6.   The word Fuck can be heard almost anywhere at anytime, not just at your local movie theatre or comedy club. Numerous other mainstream and well respected artists have used the family of fuck words in their music and performances. The Rolling Stones (who have nine number one albums, thirty-four top 10 ten [sic] albums and thirty-eight gold/platinum albums) have used the word in numerous recorded songs and hoards of additional live performances. Other popular musical artists such as Eminem, Lenny Kravitz, Tupac Shakur, Kid Rock, Busta Rhymes, 311, Bad Religion, Beck, Dr. Dre, Blink 182, Spleen Dingo and Everlast have actually titled songs that contain some variation of the word Fuck. For a complete listing of at least 417 song titles containing a member of the Fuck family, one only need access to a computer to visit the non-pornographic site inlyrics.com. Literally millions of Fucking recordings have been distributed by national recording artists, who are backed by national record label, who seem not to have a problem proliferating this prolific word and its closely related cousins. Counsel knows of no record label or record label executive that has been prosecuted for titling a band, a song or an album with a member of the Fuck family

7.   From Fa (a syllable used to represent the fourth tone of a major scale or sometimes the tone F) to Fytte (archaic version of Fit), there are roughly eight thousand six hundred words in the English language that begin with the letter F. Webster's 3rd New International Dictionary of the English Language, Unabridged, pp 811-926, (1986). Fuck has the unique distinction of being the only word commonly known as the F word. Fuck is so popular that a 272 page book entitled "The F Word" was published by the well respected national publisher Random House Books in 1999. Coincidentally, Random House also happened to be 1999's number one ranked distributor of children's books. "The F Word" is readily available at the world's largest online bookseller, Amazon.com, or your local Barnes and Noble bookseller for around fifteen dollars.

8.   A search of internet web sites suggests Fuck is a more commonly used word than mom, baseball, hot dogs, apple pie, and Chevrolet. *Google Search Engine at Google.com on June 25, 2003.*

9.   Mr. [] is alleged to have spoken two different variations of the root word Fuck. The following table depicts the number of internet search engine hits

for [] alleged "Fucker" and "Fucking" statements as compared to Fuck itself and other commonly heard words or phrases. All results are approximate.

Word	Approximate Number of Hits
Fuck	24,900,000
Fucking	24,700,000
Fucker	735,000
Mom	9,040,000
Baseball	13,600,000
Hot Dogs	607,000
Apple Pie	308,000
Chevrolet	4,090,000
Freedom of Speech	542,000
First Amendment	933,000
Unconstitutional	691,000
Sticks and Stones May Break My Bones	7,360

10. Fuck has distinct meanings based on the context in which it is used. When formally defined:

   a.   "FUCK, n. 1680

      1.   usually obscene: an act of copulation

      2.   usually obscene: a sexual partner

      3.   usually vulgar: DAMN

      4.   usually vulgar: used especially with the as a meaningless intensive <what the fuck do they want from me>"

   Merriam-Webster's Online Dictionary, www.m-w. com/cgi-bin/dictionary (emphasis in original)

   b.   The Cambridge English Readers Online Dictionary adds more zest to the definition of fuck and fucking (emphasis in original):

   "fuck (EXTREME ANGER) exclamation offensive used when express-ing extreme anger or annoyance, or to add force to what is being said:

> Fuck–the bloody car won't start!
>
> Shut the fuck up!
>
> Who the fuck does she think she is, telling me what to do?
>
> fucking adjective, adverb offensive
>
> used to emphasize a statement, especially an angry one:
>
> What a fucking waste of time!
>
> He's a fucking idiot
>
> He'd fucking better well do it."

11. Fuck possesses incredible versatility. It can be a noun (you fuck), a verb (everything Billy touches, he fucks up), an adjective (I'm really fucking broke), an adverb (I've been fucking drinking too much), an exclamation (holy fuck, Batman!) or question (what the fuck?). This versatility could partially explain the prevalence of the word and why it is so readily available to anyone with access to a computer, VCR, CD player, eight track recorder, DVD player, phonograph, cassette deck or Blockbuster Video outlet. It may explain why Fuck can be used in almost any sentence at any time no matter what the circumstance and why the word has become almost commonplace in United States culture and society.

    It is against this backdrop that we turn to the situation at hand.

12. The question presented by the case at bar is not whether Fuck is a desirable or attractive word, or whether a juvenile should be calling his principal a fucker or a fucking fag. Rather, the question is one of constitutionality and whether the State can criminalize the speech in question by application of the statute at issue. The prosecution is attempting to hold a juvenile criminally responsible for the age old tradition of name-calling. Although Mr. [] could have selected a more desirable choice in prose such as "I respectfully dissent" or "I am disappointed with your attitude sir, and politely ask you to cease and desist," the use of the words fucker and fucking nonetheless do not amount to criminal conduct in this particular context.

13. The statement alleged against Mr. [] is protected by the First and Fourteenth amendments to the United States Constitution. The United States and Colorado Constitutions both provide that no law abridging or impairing freedom of speech shall be enacted. U.S. Const. Amend. I, applies to the states through U.S. Const. Amend. XIV, and Colo. Const. Art. II, §10.

14. Freedom of thought, speech, expression and ideas are the very concepts upon which America's liberty is founded. An extremely limited number of exceptions have been judicially carved from one of the most fundamental principals [sic] of American jurisprudence. Courts have, on occasion, upheld the constitutionality of statutes which prohibit obscenity, libel, incitement, invasion of substantial privacy interests of the home and "fighting words." *People v. Hayden, 548 P.2d 1278 (Colo. 1976).*

15. Fuck is an entirely legal word that may be uttered in public places so long as the manner in which it is uttered will not cause a violent reaction. *Cohen v. California[,] 403 U.S. 15 (1971)[.]("Fuck the Draft" jacket worn in a courthouse was protected by the [F]irst [A]mendment).* In overturning a disorderly conduct conviction, the Cohen Court went on to state:

Against this perception of the constitutional policies involved, we discern certain more particularized considerations that peculiarly call for reversal of this conviction. First, the principle contended for by the State seems inherently boundless. How is one to distinguish this from any other offensive word? Surely the State has no right to cleanse public debate to the point where it is grammatically palatable to the most squeamish among us. Yet no readily ascertainable general principle exists for stopping short of that result were we to affirm the judgment below. For, while the particular four-letter word being litigated here is perhaps more distasteful than most others of its genre, it is nevertheless often true *that one man's vulgarity is another's lyric. Indeed, we think it is largely because governmental officials cannot make principled distinctions in this area that the Constitution leaves matters of taste and style so largely to the individual.* Additionally, we cannot overlook the fact, because it is well illustrated by the episode involved here, that much linguistic expression serves a dual communicative function: it conveys not only ideas capable of relatively precise, detached explication, but otherwise inexpressible emotions as well. In fact, words are often chosen as much for their emotive as their cognitive force. We cannot sanction the view that the Constitution, while solicitous of the cognitive content of individual speech, has little or no regard for that emotive function which, practically speaking, may often be the more important element of the overall message sought to be communicated. Indeed, as Mr. Justice Frankfurter has said, "[o]ne of the prerogatives of American citizenship is the right to criticize public men and measures—and that means not only informed and responsible criticism but the freedom to speak foolishly and without moderation." Baumgartner v. United States, 322 U.S. 665, 673-674 (1944). Finally, and in the same vein, we cannot indulge the facile assumption that one can forbid particular words without also running a substantial risk of suppressing ideas in the process. Indeed, governments might soon seize upon the censorship of particular words as a convenient guise for banning the expression of unpopular views. We have been able, as noted above, to discern little social benefit that might result from running the risk of opening the door to such grave results.

Cohen at 25-26. (emphasis added)

16. The Colorado Supreme Court used the same reasoning in citing and following Cohen by overturning a municipal conviction based on the defendant, Mr. Wade, yelling "Fuck You" at a meeting of over two hundred people at the University of Denver campus. *Ware v. City and County of Denver*, 511 P.2d 475 (Colo. 1973).

17. The statement "I don't need this fuckin' school anyway" in concert with violently slamming a door was found to be constitutionally protected speech. The statement was made by a juvenile to a police officer in a school setting after the juvenile was called to the principal's office to be informed that she was being expelled from school. *L.M.A.W. v. State, 611 So.2d 497 (Ala. Cr. App. 1992) (conviction for disorderly conduct overturned).*

18. "Shut the fuck up" and words to the effect of "don't let the door hit you on the ass on the way out" were ruled to be constitutionally protected speech. *B.E.S. v. State, 629 So.2d 761 (Ala. Cr. App. 1993).*

19. A juvenile telling a police officer "fuck you" was held to be constitutionally protected speech. *R.I.T. v State, 675 So.2d 97 (Ala. Cr. App. 1995) (conviction for disorderly conduct overturned).* The *R.I.T.* court reasoned that police officers are specially trained to deal with vulgarities and situations when others may be verbally abusive towards them, and thus "fuck you" was not likely to provoke a violent response.

20. A juvenile calling a police officer a "fucking pig, fucking kangaroo" and telling the officer "fuck you" during a traffic contact was found to be constitutionally protected speech. *State v. John W., 418 A.2d 1097 (Me. 1980)*. Just like the *R.I.T.* court, *Id.*, the *John W.* court also reasoned that police officers deal with these types of situations on an every day basis and therefore "fucking pig, fucking kangaroo and fuck you" were not likely to invoke a violent response.

21. Finally, the Arizona case of *In Re Louise C.* is almost directly on point with the case at bar. Louise C. was brought to the principal's office in relation to a conflict with another student. In the presence of the other student, the principal, and the vice-principal, Louise C. was asked whether she planned to fight the other student. She lashed out and said "Fuck this, I don't have to take this shit" and walked toward the door. When the principal asked her to stop she said "Fuck you, I don't have to do what you tell me" and slammed the door behind her. She was later suspended for school for the incident. Louise C.'s statements and conduct were found to be constitutionally protected by the First Amendment. *In Re Louise C., 3 P.2d 1004 (Az. App. 1999)*.

22. The state has the power to protect its citizenry from actual harm, and thus has the power to outlaw one yelling "Fire!" in a crowded theatre. *See, Schenck v. United States, 249 U.S. 47 (1919)*. However, yelling "Fuck!" in a crowded theatre does not create a clear and present danger to anyone and thus cannot be outlawed. Although they are both four letter words that start with F, the distinction is constitutionally significant.[283]

23. The elements of Interference with Staff, Faculty or Students of Educational Institutions require proof beyond a reasonable doubt that Mr. [] unlawfully and willfully impeded the staff and faculty of the school. The elements also require that he do so by using restraint, abduction, coercion or intimidation. It is difficult to imagine how calling one's principal some naughty words hinder his ability to do his job. Although counsel has not seen a formal description of what his job requires, typically a principal is called on to deal with situations precisely like the one at hand. This is surely not the first time the principal has heard an offensive remark or been called a bad name. In contrast to the general public, one would expect a principal to have special training in dealing with situations that require non-criminal discipline and reprimand. In fact, rather than violently responding to the insults, the prin-

cipal suspended Mr. [] from school for the incident in question, an entirely legal and appropriate reaction to the alleged statements. However, criminal charges and the potential sanctions that come along with them are categorically different than the in-house sanctions that Mr. [] already suffered.

24. Fuck is certainly a controversial word that may be appropriate in certain venues and locales (Florida Elections Commission, speed eating contests, public defender offices) and may be inappropriate in others (weddings, Chuck-E-Cheese pizza parlors, district attorney offices). Some people believe it is always inappropriate. But in all but a very few circumstances, the First Amendment to the United States Constitution prohibits our government from making that determination. This case falls outside of those very limited circumstances and as such, no conviction can result from Mr. [] alleged statements.

Therefore, the Court must dismiss this case.

DAVID S. KAPLAN
COLORADO STATE PUBLIC DEFENDER

[signature omitted]
ERIC VANATTA [# omitted]
Deputy State Public Defender

Conclusion

In the grand scheme, America is experimental-theater to the time-tested dramas of Europe, Asia, Africa and the Middle East. We are governed by a relatively brief document drafted by wealthy farmers in an Agrarian society, challenged by the advent of Industrialization, and now attempting to "plug itself in" to the Information age brought on by a dramatic technological revolution.

To sum up my "observations" herein, I assert that the U.S. Constitution doesn't always do what people want it to. A law that is "constitutional," might, at the same time, be unnecessary, poor policy, or even silly. Is this a good law and is this constitutional are not the same question. There are many laws I would urge my representatives in Congress to oppose or vote against as referendum if given the chance that are, nonetheless, constitutional and thus not contrary to the U.S. Constitution in such a way that the Court must strike them down. The Supreme Court is not a branch of representative government and its role in exercising "judicial review" should be coupled with one of deep judicial restraint as one of three branches in a supposedly "limited" federal government. The relevant inquiry is: does the Constitution afford to an individual a right that is being infringed upon by a given statute which is subject to judicial review? This restraint should be especially great in cases involving the First Amendment as it is written in absolute terms as a restriction on Congress. However, this has not been the case, and the single Amendment written clearly as a limit on the *most* representative branch of our government, has been expanded to govern by a series of incoherent balancing tests wholly created by our *least* democratic branch of government.

Overall, I espouse that the mere existence of the obscenity doctrine is constitutionally flawed in light of the static language of the First Amendment. However, given the apparently permanent existence of this and other such ill-advised "balancing tests," the parameters of the *Miller*-test should not themselves be content-based and skewed to provide an inevitable result. Similarly, I shudder to think of flooding our overly-litigious society with endless tort lawsuits aimed at works of extreme speech and expression. The aim of such measures may well be desirable but must be sought by legitimate, democratic means.

The primary premise of my argument is that the current state of our First Amendment has been shaped by the courts and not the People. The courts have "balanced" an individual right that is static and, if interpreted as written, does not allow balancing at all. While the express language of certain Amendments, such as the Fourth Amendment's fluid "reasonableness" requirement or the subjective terms "cruel and unusual" in the Eighth Amendment may allow for such balancing, nothing in the First Amendment invites or allows such manipulation.

If such lawsuits should be curbed to avoid perceived "chill," if "obscene" materials (whether sexual or not) should be banned, if a broader separation of church and state is desirable, this should be the result of representative government (*via* constitutional amendment or other legislative process) and not through the expansive wizardry of the interpretive arm of the federal courts.[284]

About the Author

Attorney **Marc M. Harrold**, a visiting professor at the University of Mississippi School of Law, is the author of numerous works of legal nonfiction. He lives in Union County, Mississippi.

Endnotes

[1] U.S. Const. preamble

[2] Quote used with permission from Professor Blasi, University of Virginia School of Law.

[3] "There is plenty of room within [the American] system for 'evolving standards of decency,' but the instrument of evolution (or, if you are more tolerant of the Court's approach, the herald that evolution has occurred) is not the nine lawyers who sit on the Supreme Court of the United States, but the Congress of the United States and the legislatures of the fifty states,...." Antonin Scalia, remarks made during a conference sponsored by the Pew Forum on Religion and Public Life at the University of Chicago Divinity School.

[4] 413 U.S. 15 (1973).

[5] *Miller,* 413 U.S. at 39–41 (Douglas, J., dissenting).

[6] 60 U.S. 393 (1857). Actually the man's name was John *Sanford,* not John *Sandford*—a clerk misspelled the name and it was never corrected. PETER IRONS, *A PEOPLE'S HISTORY OF THE SUPREME COURT,* Penguin Group at 163 (1999).

[7] Unfortunately, this is not always the case. A prime example is found in *Dickerson v. United States,* 530 U.S. 428 (2000), where the Supreme Court held that the warning-based approach announced in *Miranda* was not a prophylactic measure of the Fourth Amendment, but amounted to a "constitutional rule that Congress may not supercede legislatively." *Dickerson,* 520 U.S. at 444. Chief Justice Rehnquist authored the opinion; it was not his finest moment. Justice Scalia, in dissent, recognized the arrogance of the decision:

> Today's judgment converts *Miranda* from the milestone of judicial overreaching into the very Cheops' Pyramid (or perhaps the Sphinx would be a better analogue) of judicial arrogance. In imposing its Court-made code upon the States, the original opinion at least *asserted* that it was demanded by the Constitution. Today's decision does not pretend that it is—and yet *still* asserts the right to impose it against the will of the people's representatives in Congress. Far from believing *stare decisis* compels this result, I believe we cannot allow to remain on the books even a celebrated decision—*especially* a celebrated decision—that has come to stand for the proposition that the Supreme Court has power to impose extraconstitutional constraints upon Congress and the States.

This is not the system that was established by the Framers, or that would be established by any sane supporter of government by the people.

Id. at 465 (Scalia, J., dissenting). *See also Katz v. United States*, 389 U.S. 347, 364–65 (1967) (Black, J., dissenting) (referring to Court's interpretation of Fourth Amendment).

My basic objection is twofold: (1) I do not believe that the words of the Amendment will bear the meaning given them by today's decision, and (2) I do not believe that it is the proper role of this Court to rewrite the Amendment in order 'to bring it into harmony with the times' and thus reach a result that many people believe to be desirable.

...

While I realize that an argument based on the meaning of the words lacks the scope, and no doubt the appeal, of broad policy discussions and philosophical discourses on such nebulous subjects as privacy, for me the language of the Amendment is the crucial place to look in construing a written document such as our Constitution.

Id. (Black, J., dissenting).

[8] While the text of the First Amendment is directed only towards the federal government, (specifically only "Congress") the Fourteenth Amendment has acted to "incorporate" the First Amendment to the states. Although the most logical place in the Fourteenth Amendment for such "incorporation" to be rooted is the "privileges or immunities" Clause, the U.S. Supreme Court has instead couched this "incorporation" of the Bill of Rights within the reference to "liberty" found in the Due Process Clause of the Fourteenth Amendment. *See, e.g., Stromberg v. California*, 283 U.S. 359, 368 (1931) ("It has been determined that the conception of liberty under the due process clause of the Fourteenth Amendment embraces the right of free speech."), citing *Gitlow v. New York*, 268 U.S. 652, 666 (1925); *Whitney v. California*, 274 U.S. 357, 362, 371, 373 (1927); *Fiske v. Kansas*, 274 U.S. 380, 382 (1927) (speech). *See also Near v. Minnesota*, 283 U.S. 697, 701 (1931) (Press); *De Jonge v. Oregon*, 299 U.S. 353, 364 (1937) (Assembly); *Edwards v. South Carolina*, 372 U.S. 229, 235 (1963) (Petition); *Cantwell v. Connecticut*, 310 U.S. 296, 303 (1940) (Free Exercise Clause); *Illinois ex rel. McCollum v. Board of Educ.*, 333 U.S. 203, 211 (1948) (Establishment Clause).

[9] Regardless of one's opinion as to whether this was intended only towards members of a militia.

[10] Some scholars do not find the "Congress"-only distinction found in the First Amendment, but not in the other Amendments to have any significant value. "It seems to have been routine for the Constitutionalists of 1789 to consider restraints upon Congress to be restraints as well upon the rest of the General Government." GEORGE ANASTAPLO, THE AMENDMENTS TO THE CONSTITUTION—A COMMENTARY 49 (The John Hopkins University Press 1995).

[11] *See e.g.,* Donald A. Dripps, *The Fourth Amendment and the Fallacy of Composition: Determinacy Versus Legitimacy in a Regime of Bright-Line Rules,* 74 MISS. L.J. 341 (Special Ed. 2004) ("The language of the Fourth Amendment is among the most spacious in the Constitution."). In comparison, I do not believe that the language of the First Amendment is "spacious" at all. *See also* AMITAI ETZIONI, HOW PATRIOTIC IS THE PATRIOT ACT? 4 (Routledge 2004) ("[The Fourth Amendment] is not phrased in terms as absolute as the First Amendment. It does not state that Congress "shall make no law allowing search and seizure.").

[12] The Fourth Amendment also contains the fluid term "probable" which is properly open to interpretation.

[13] I used the *"CRS Report for Congress—received through the CRS Web—Freedom of Speech and Press: Exceptions to the First Amendment"* written by Henry Cohen, Legislative Attorney, American Law Division, updated Nov. 5, 2001 as a major resource for this section. *See also Chaplinksy v. New Hampshire,* 315 U.S. 568, 571–72 (1942) ("There are certain well-defined and narrowly limited classes of speech, the prevention and punishment of which has never been thought to raise any Constitutional problem.").

[14] *Miller,* 413 U.S. at 27.

[15] *Id.* The three (3) prongs of the *Miller*-test are not interpreted in exactly the same manner: "[T]he first and second prongs of the Miller test—appeal to prurient interest and patent offensiveness—are issues of fact for the jury to determine applying contemporary community standards." *Pope v. Illinois,* 481 U.S. 497, 500 (1987). For the third prong, "[t]he proper inquiry is not whether an ordinary member of any given community would find serious literary, artistic, political or scientific value in allegedly obscene material, but whether a reasonable person would find such value in the material, taken as a whole." *Id.* at 500-01.

[16] Prurient Interest is defined by Black's Law Dictionary (6th Ed.) as "[a] shameful or morbid interest in nudity, sex, or excretion." Model Penal Code § 251.4(1). An obsessive interest in immoral and lascivious matters. An excessive or

unnatural interest in sex. [the definition goes on to acknowledge that "prurient interest" is part of the *Miller*-test for determining obscenity.]

[17] *Miller*, 413 U.S. at 24.

[18] *Stanley v. Georgia*, 394 U.S. 557, 568 (1969).

[19] 458 U.S. 747 (1982).

[20] *Osborne v. Ohio*, 495 U.S. 103 (1990).

[21] *Chaplinsky v. State of New Hampshire*, 315 U.S. 568, 572 (1942).

[22] 395 U.S. 444 (1969) (*per curium*)

[23] *Brandenburg*, 395 U.S. at 447.

[24] *Watts v. United States*, 394 U.S. 705, 708 (1969) (*per curium*).

[25] *R.A.V. v. City of St. Paul*, 505 U.S. 377 (1992). *See also* Madsen v. *Women's Health Center, Inc.*, 512 U.S. 753, 774 (1994); *Scheck v. Pro-Choice Network of Western N.Y.*, 519 U.S. 357, 373 (1997).

[26] "Actual malice" in this context means "with knowledge that it was false or with reckless disregard of whether it was false or not." *See New York Times v. Sullivan*, 376 U.S. 254, 279–80 (1964); *Curtis Publishing Co. v Butts*, 388 U.S. 130 (1967).

[27] Although not necessarily actual malice.

[28] *Gertz v. Robert Welch, Inc.*, 418 U.S. 323 (1974).

[29] *Valentine v. Chrestensen*, 316 U.S. 52, 52–55 (1952).

[30] 447 U.S. 557 (1980) ((a) protected speech; (b) substantial governmental interest; (c) interest "directly advanced"; and (d) means-end fit)

[31] I think that it was a commercial for *Prevacid* but I can't remember for sure.

[32] Obviously, I don't really think the animated stomach is, or should be, legally obscene in any way, but it made me think.

[33] 413 U.S. 15, 20 (1973).

[34] *Id.* at 43 (Douglas, J., dissenting). Justice Hugo Black did not believe that an "exception" such as the one for obscenity was consistent with the First Amendment. *See Ginzburg v. United States*, 383 U.S. 463, 476 (Black, J., dissenting) ("[T]he Federal Government is without any power whatever under the Constitution to put any type of burden on speech and expression of ideas of any kind.") *See also Ashcroft v. ACLU*, 542 U.S. 656, 690 (2004) ("I recognize that some Members of the Court, now or in the past, have taken the view that the First Amendment simply does not permit Congress to legislate in this area") (Breyer, J., dissenting).

[35] *Jacobellis v. Ohio*, 378 U.S. 184, 197 (Stewart, J., concurring) (emphasis added).

[36] 413 U.S. 15 (1973).

[37] A good example of the First Amendment's under-inclusiveness prohibition is found in *R.A.V. v. St Paul*, 505 U.S. 377 (1992). The Court struck down what would have been basically a valid "fighting words" statute because the statute was limited to certain motivations:

> Applying these principles to the St. Paul ordinance, we conclude that, even as narrowly construed by the Minnesota Supreme Court, the ordinance is facially unconstitutional. Although the phrase in the ordinance, "arouses anger, alarm or resentment in others," has been limited by the Minnesota Supreme Court's construction to reach only those symbols or displays that amount to "fighting words," the remaining, unmodified terms make clear that the ordinance applies only to "fighting words" that insult, or provoke violence, "on the basis of race, color, creed, religion or gender." Displays containing abusive invective, no matter how vicious or severe, are permissible unless they are addressed to one of the specified disfavored topics. Those who wish to use "fighting words" in connection with other ideas—to express hostility, for example, on the basis of political affiliation, union membership, or homosexuality—are not covered. The First Amendment does not permit St. Paul to impose special prohibitions on those speakers who express views on disfavored subjects. See Simon & Schuster, 502 U.S., at 116 ; Arkansas Writers' Project, Inc. v. Ragland, 481 U.S. 221, 229 -230 (1987).

R.A.V., 505 U.S. at 391. In the case of the obscenity-test found in *Miller*, it appears that this balancing test, while not actually a statute, acts in a similarly "under-inclusive" and "content-restrictive" manner. The policy in *Miller* is to allow individual communities to deem certain speech to be "super-offensive" and thus outside of the ambit of First Amendment protections. The test set forth in Miller goes one-step further in holding that even if different examples of speech reach this level of "super-offensiveness," only those that involve sex (or prurient interest) can be deemed offensive and fall outside the boundaries of full constitutional protection. This is the part of the balancing-test that is "under-inclusive" and treats an overall category of speech that meets similar requirements (*i.e.* "fighting words in the *R.A.V.* case and "super-offensiveness" in the case of obscenity) differently based on the content of the speech.

[38] *Miller*, 413 U.S. at 24. The test set forth in *Miller* for obscenity: The basic guidelines for the trier of fact must be: (a) whether "the average person, applying contemporary community standards" would find that the work, taken as a whole, appeals to the prurient interest, (b) whether the work depicts or describes, in a patently offensive way, sexual conduct specifically defined by the applicable state

law, and (c) whether the work, taken as a whole, lacks serious literary, artistic, political or scientific value. *Id.*

[39] 403 U.S. 15 (1971). The Court, in *Cohen*, stated "[w]hatever else may be necessary to give rise to the States' broader power to prohibit obscene expression, such expression must be, in some significant way, erotic." *Cohen*, 403 U.S. at 20.

[40] Referring to the "damned if you do…damned if you don't" literary cliché emerging from Joseph Heller's classic novel *Catch 22*.

[41] 244 F.3d 572 (7th Cir. 2001).

[42] *Id.* Justice Posner has some history dealing with Indianapolis statutes challenged before the Seventh Circuit on First Amendment grounds. Previously Justice Posner vigorously dissented in an opinion dealing with an Indianapolis statute banning all-nude dancing within the city limits and requiring erotic dancers to wear pasties and G-strings.

[43] *Id.* at 575.

[44] The Indianapolis statute at issue in *American Amusement Machine v. Kendrick* basically attempts to add violent content by criminalizing video games that are, "harmful to minors." *American Amusement Machine*, 244 F.3d at 573. The "harmful to minors" standard in the Indianapolis statute is the test set forth in *Miller* for prurient interest plus proscription of "graphic violence." *Id.*

> "Harmful to minors," in relation to video games means, "an amusement machine that predominantly appeals to minors' morbid interest in violence or minors' prurient interest in sex, is patently offensive to prevailing standards in the adult community as a whole with respect with what is suitable material for persons under the age of eighteen (18) years, lacks serious literary, artistic, scientific value as a whole for persons under" that age and contains either "graphic violence" or "strong sexual content."

Id.

[45] *Id.* "[b]ut in general the concerns [obscenity and offensiveness] are different. The main worry about obscenity, the main reason for its proscription, is not that it is harmful, which is the worry behind the Indianapolis ordinance, but that it is offensive." *Id.*

[46] *Video Software Dealers Assoc. v. Maleng*, 325 F. Supp. 2d 1180, 1185 (W.D. Wash. 2004).

[47] Peter Schweizer, *Bad Imitation*, NAT'L REV., Dec. 1998, at 23.

[48] *Olivia N. v. National Broadcasting Co., Inc.*, 74 Cal. App. 3d 383, 386, 141 Cal. Rptr. 511, 512 (1977).

[49] This individual scene is used in this context for illustrative purposes only. There is a good chance that the third prong of *Miller* would determine that the overall film has "artistic" value and therefore the film as a whole would not be obscene. As we will explore later in this chapter, this would be true of either the existing *Miller*-doctrine (under the third prong) or my proposed content-neutral obscenity doctrine. *See also Ashcroft v. Free Speech Coalition*, 535 U.S. 234, 248 (2002) ("The artistic merit of a work does not depend on the presence of one explicit scene."). "Under *Miller*, the First Amendment requires that redeeming value be judged by considering the work as a whole. Where the scene is part of the narrative, the work itself does not for this reason become obscene, even though the scene in isolation might be offensive." *Id.* at 248. (additional citation omitted).

[50] *Interactive Digital Software Ass'n v. St. Louis County, Missouri*, 329 F.3d 954, 958 (8th Cir. 2003) (citing *Winters v. New York*, 333 U.S. 507, 510, 68 S. Ct. 665, 92 L. Ed. 840 (1948)).

[51] *Video Sotftware Dealers Assoc. v. Maleng*, 325 F. Supp. 2d 1180, 1183 (W.D. Wash. 2004). *See also American Amusement Mach. Ass'n v. Kendrick*, 244 F.3d 572 (7th Cir. 2001); *Video Software Dealers Ass'n v. Webster*, 968 F.2d 684 (8th Cir. 1992); *James v. Meow Media, Inc.*, 300 F.3d 683 (6th Cir. 2002) (tort liability fails in light of First Amendment); *Wilson v. Midway Games, Inc.*, 198 F. Supp. 2d 167 (D. Conn. 2002) (same); *Sanders v. Acclaim Entm't Inc.*, 188 F. Supp. 2d 1264 (D. Colo. 2002) (same).

[52] *Maleng*, 325 F. Supp. 2d at 1185.

[53] *See* www.churchofeuthanasia.com.

[54] *Id.*

[55] Rebecca Sinderbrand, "*Point, Click and Die—'Pro-choice' suicide sites come under legal scrutiny*," NEWSWEEK, June 30, 2003 at 28.

[56] *Id.*

[57] 458 U.S. 747, 758 (1982). Generally, pornography can only be banned if it is obscene. Under *Ferber*, pornography showing minors can be banned whether or not the images can also be classified as obscene under *Miller*.

[58] 535 U.S. 234, 239 (2002). I deal with "virtual" child pornography in the context of the Internet. It appears that this analysis could be equally relevant where images are created with the use of a computer and traded without the use of the Internet, or the use of adults to portray minors in sexual activity is used to create images that either do not utilize computer technology or are never transmitted over the Internet.

[59] *See, e.g.,* www.barelylegal.com. Adult women are made to look younger in a variety of ways including costumes, shaving of pubic hair, and other measures to eliminate or minimize adult secondary sexual characteristics.

> Despite the predictable objections of conservatives, feminists and parents worried they might see their daughters doing the nasty on a rental, *Barely Legal,* with all of its cock-teasing, barrette-wearing, teddy bear-hugging teen love, is only the most lurid form of a society-wide obsession with young girls. For example, the December 1999 issue of Bob Guccione Jr.'s non-porn men's mag *Gear* features 17-year-old actress Kirsten Dunst in a photo-spread/cover story that offers this bit of crumpet up, variously in panties, a bikini and a tiger-print slip. Similarly the current *Rolling Stone* has the barely legal, 19-year-old Christina Ricci on the cover in lingerie. Inside, Ricci is featured sitting on a bed, showing off her cavernous cleavage and looking particularly girlish with a large pair of mouse ears on her head.
>
> There are also TV shows like "Buffy the Vampire Slayer," "Sabrina the Teenage Witch" and "Time of Your Life," whose girl-protagonists could easily be potential porn starlets in a *Barely Legal* video. You can gauge their sex appeal by how many times the actresses who portray them appear in their underwear on the cover of *Maxim* or in "Got Milk?" ads.
>
> Then there's the recent film "American Beauty," in which Kevin Spacey's cynical suburban dad comes oh so very close to deflowering Mena Suvari's decadent, pom-pom-waving teen minx. And as far as the Internet is concerned: Everyone knows, anything goes. You can even get streaming video of teens having sex coming from such places as Russia or Amsterdam, if you are so inclined.
>
> Ecclesiastes states that there's nothing new under the sun. Along these lines, Vladimir Nabokov's "Lolita" comes to mind, as do the paintings of Balthus and the less edifying Brooke Shields vehicles "Blue Lagoon" and "Endless Love." Furthermore, history and religion are filled with too many tales of child brides to even mention. Even in the age of consent in the United States varies according to state, running anywhere from as low as 13 (in New Mexico, with certain restrictions) to as high as 18 elsewhere.

Available at www.salon.com/health/sex/urge/1999/12/04/underage/print.html (last visited April 11, 2005) (emphasis added).

[60] *See generally Ashcroft v. Free Speech Coalition,* 535 U.S. 234 (2002).

[61] Quoted directly from an e-mail from Detective Rick Hardy on or about August 8, 2003. Reprinted with permission.

[62] Reprinted with permission from Dr. Hany Farid, Department of Computer Science, Dartmouth College. Quote reprinted from e-mail sent directly from Dr. Farid to Author (Oct. 13, 2004).

[63] *Ashcroft*, 535 U.S. at 240.

[64] 458 U.S. 747 (1982).

[65] *Ferber*, 458 U.S. at 758.

[66] *Ashcroft*, 535 U.S. at 239 ("The CPPA extends the federal prohibition against child pornography to sexually explicit images that appear to depict minors but were produced without using any real children.")

[67] *Id.* at 240.

[68] *Id.* at 246.

[69] *Id.*

[70] The textbook would also not be obscene under a content-neutral obscenity doctrine because of the continued viability of the third prong of the *Miller*-test (detailed in a separate section). It seems clear that a psychology manual, as a whole, would have serious scientific value.

[71] The A&F Quarterly "Christmas Field Guide" that caused all the controversy featured the banner "280 Pages of Moose, Ice Hockey, Chivalry, Group Sex & More..."

[72] 771 F.2d 323 (7th Cir. 1985).

[73] *Hudnut*, 771 F.2d at 324.

[74] *Id.*

[75] *Id.* at 324–25 (citing Catharine A. MacKinnon, *Pornography, Civil Rights, and Speech*, 20 HARV. CIV. RTS.—CIV. LIB. L. REV. 1, 21 (1985)).

[76] *Hudnut*, 771 F.2d at 328.

[77] *Miller*, 413 U.S. at 24.

[78] This Section will cover "words" generally, either in printed form or in the form of musical lyrics. Basically, words (or lyrics) not accompanied by specific visual imagery are covered.

[79] *Davidson v. Time Warner, Inc.*, No. Civ. 94-006, 1997 WL 405907 (S.D. Tex. Mar. 31, 1997) (case not reported in F. Supp.).

[80] *Id.* at *2 n. 4.

[81] *Davidson v. Time Warner, Inc.*, No. Civ. 94-006, 1997 WL 405907 (S.D. Tex. Mar. 31, 1997).

[82] *Id.* at *22. (emphasis added).

[83] *Id.*

[84] There is a chance that, even under a doctrine of content-neutral obscenity the third-prong of Miller would hold that rap music has serious political value and is

does not fall outside the protections of the First Amendment. *See, e.g.,* Robert
Firester and Kendall T. Jones, *Catchin' the Heat of the Beat: First Amendment
Analysis of Music Claimed to Incite Violent Behavior,* 20 LOY. L.A. ENT. L. REV. 2
(2000) ("Could gangsta rap fall into the category of "political speech" and
thereby receive the highest level of judicial protection?")

[85] Original quote from an e-mail from Dean Rodney Smolla to author, August 7,
2003.

[86] The book was written by "Rex Ferral" and published by Paladin Press. Rex Ferral is a pen name, the author of the book was actually female.

[87] The book begins with the following: "WARNING—IT IS AGAINST THE
LAW TO manufacture a silencer without an appropriate license from the federal
government. There are state and local laws prohibiting the possession of weapons
and their accessories in many areas. Severe penalties are prescribed for violations
of these laws. Neither the author nor the publisher assumes responsibility for the
use or misuse of information contained in this book. **For informational purposes only!**" [cite not available]

[88] *See Miller,* 413 U.S. at 44 (Douglas, J., dissenting) ("There is no 'captive audience' problem in these obscenity cases. No one is being compelled to look or to
listen. Those who enter newsstands or bookstalls may be offended by what they
see. But they are not compelled by the State to frequent those places; and it is
only state or governmental action against which the First Amendment, applicable
to the States by the Fourteenth, raises a ban.")

[89] In his article, *Unholy Fire: Cross Burning, Symbolic Speech, and the First Amendment* Virginia v. Black, James Swanson makes an interesting observation about
the place of fire in traditional American expression:

> Of all mediums of symbolic expression, Americans have displayed an especial
> affection for fire. Throughout our history we have burned things to communi-
> cate a message. Hanging and burning in effigy one's enemies was a traditional,
> albeit alarming, form of American political protest, particularly in the eigh-
> teenth and nineteenth centuries. In 1794, when John Jay returned to the
> United States after negotiating the unpopular treaty that bears his name, he
> was so vilified that he said that he could find his way home in the dark from
> the number of burning effigies that illuminated the roads.

[90] *See* University of Southern California/USC Law: News (available at http://
lawweb.usc.edu/news/releases/Johnson.htm) (visited Aug. 11, 2003).

[91] *Texas v. Johnson,* 491 U.S. 397, 399 (1989).

[92] *See Miller*, 413 U.S. at 29 ("But today, for the first time since Roth was decided in 1957, a majority of this Court has agreed on concrete guidelines to isolate 'hard-core' pornography from expression protected by the First Amendment.")

[93] 491 U.S. 397 (1989).

[94] *See Johnson*, 491 U.S. at 400 n. 1. ("Texas Penal Code Ann. § 42.09 (1989) provides in full:

"§42.09 Desecration of Venerated object

(a) A person commits an offense if he intentionally or knowingly desecrates:

(1) a public monument;

(2) a place of worship or burial; or

(3) a state or national flag.

(b) For purposes of this section, 'desecrate' means deface, damage, or otherwise physically mistreat in a way that the actor knows will seriously offend one or more persons likely to observe or discover his action.

(c) An offense under this Section is a Class A misdemeanor.")

[95] *Johnson*, 491 U.S. at 420. Chief Justice Rehnquist, in dissent, criticizes the Majority opinion as being "patronizing." *Id.* at 434 (Rehnquist, C.J., dissenting) ("The Court concludes its opinion with a regrettably patronizing civics lecture, presumably addressed to the Members of both Houses of Congress, the members of the 48 state legislatures that enacted prohibitions against flag burning, and the troops fighting under that flag in Vietnam who objected to its being burned: [text omitted]…[t]he Court's role as the final expositor of the Constitution is well established, but its role as a Platonic guardian admonishing those responsible to public opinion as if they were truant school-children has no similar place in our system of government.")

[96] *Johnson*, 491 U.S. at 420.

[97] *Id.* at 417.

[98] *Id.* at 420.

[99] *Id.*

[100] As always, there is a somewhat circular nature to the obscenity doctrine with regards to flag-burning (and possibly even cross-burning) because the third-prong of *Miller* could deem that the speech-conduct in question, as a whole, is not lacking political value.

[101] James L. Swanson, *Unholy Fire: Cross Burning, Symbolic Speech, and the First Amendment* Virginia v. Black, CATO SUPREME COURT REVIEW at 89 (2003).

[102] 123 S. Ct. 1536 (2003).

[103] *Id.* The Virginia cross-burning statute § 18.2-423 provides:

It shall be unlawful for any person or persons, with the intent of intimidating any person or group of persons, to burn, or cause to be burned, a cross on the property of another, a highway or other public place. Any person who shall violate any provision of this section shall be guilty of a Class 6 felony.

Any such burning of a cross shall be prima facie evidence of an intent to intimidate a person or group of persons.

[104] 505 U.S. 377 (1992).

[105] *Virginia v. Black*, 538 U.S. 343, 362 (2003).

[106] *Chaplinsky v. New Hampshire*, 315 U.S. 568, 571–72 (1942).

[107] *Watts v. United States*, 394 U.S. 705, 708 (1969) (*per curium*).

[108] A large portion of the ruling in *Virginia v. Black* surrounded the second section of the statute which states, "[a]ny such burning of a cross shall be prima facie evidence of an intent to intimidate a person or group of persons." This legislative attempt to "impute" intent is acknowledged but not covered herein.

[109] *Black*, 538 U.S. 343, 391 (Thomas, J., dissenting) (internal citations omitted).

[110] The Court, in *Virginia v. Black*, expressly noted the obscenity doctrine as an example where the government could "'choose to prohibit only that obscenity which is the most patently offensive *in its prurience—i.e,* that which involves the most lascivious displays of sexual activity.'" *Black*, 538 U.S. at 362 (citations omitted). It is not clear if the Court is recognizing that some obscene materials might not be sexual.

[111] *Black*, 538 U.S. at 366.

[112] *Id.* at 348.

[113] *Id.* at 367.

[114] Justice Thomas, in dissent, believes that the "majority errs in imputing an expressive component to the activity in question…."

[115] *Black*, 538 U.S. at 388 (Thomas, J., dissenting). "In my view, whatever expressive value cross burning has, the legislature simply wrote it out by banning only intimidating conduct undertaken by a particular means. A conclusion that the statute prohibiting cross burning with intent to intimidate sweeps beyond a prohibition on certain conduct into the zone of expression overlooks not only the words of the statute but also reality." *Id.* (Thomas, J., dissenting).

[116] *Black*, 538 U.S. at 381 (Souter, J., concurring in part; dissenting in part).

[117] *Texas,* 109 S. Ct. at 2539. (internal quotations omitted).

[118] *Id.* (internal quotations omitted) (emphasis added).

[119] It should be remembered that the Virginia statute in question only criminalizes cross burning which takes place "on the property of another, a highway or

other public place." *See* Va. Code Ann. § 18.2-423 (1996). If a cross burning is done in private without an audience for reasons of, let's say, White Protestant solidarity, this law does not apply. In situations where there is an audient, even if the intent is not to intimidate, there is very little likelihood that any other message will be received, and thus, the First Amendment is not even brought "into play."

[120] *Lawrence v. Texas*, 539 U.S. 558, 562 (2003) (emphasis added). For a good example of the intersection of the concepts of "liberty" and "free speech," generally, see, *Bose Corp. v. Consumers Union of U.S, Inc.*, 466 U.S. 485, 503–04 (1984) ("The First Amendment presupposes that the freedom to speak one's mind is not only an aspect of individual liberty—and thus a good unto itself—but also is essential to the common quest for truth and the vitality of society as a whole.").

[121] *See supra*, note 15 and accompanying text.

[122] *See generally* Marc M. Harrold, *"The Cyber-Community Jones's Can't Keep up With the Miller[s]: The 'Community Standards' Doctrine in the Age of the Internet and its Effect on E-Commerce,"* THE INTERNET L.J., Dec. 26, 2000.

[123] *Salt Lake City v. Piepenburg*, 571 P.2d 1299, 1299–1300 (Utah 1977) (case red-flagged).

[124] *Ashcroft*, 535 U.S. at 246.

[125] *Video Software Dealers Assoc. v. Maleng*, 325 F. Supp. 2d 1180, 1185 (W.D. Wash. 2004).

[126] *Id.*

[127] *Baker v. Glover*, 776 F. Supp. 1511, 1515 (M.D. Ala. 1991).

[128] *Members of City Council v. Taxpayers for Vincent*, 466 U.S. 789, 812 n. 30 (1984).

[129] The State of Alabama argued that the bumper sticker was not constitutionally protected speech because (1) it is obscene as to adults; (2) it is obscene as to children; (3) its message constitutes "fighting words"; and (4) it is likely to distract motorists and as a result interfere with highway safety.

[130] *Baker*, 776 F. Supp. at 1515.

[131] *Id.*

[132] *Id.* (internal citations omitted)

[133] *Id.*

[134] *Id.* (emphasis added).

[135] *Smith v. California*, 361 U.S. 147, 160 (1959) (Black, J., concurring)

[136] *See supra*, note 110 and accompanying text.

[137] July 13, 2001—speaking in New Orleans, Louisiana.

[138] This would apply equally to state governments after the complicated "incorporation" of the Bill of Rights to the states through the 14th Amendment. A full explanation and analysis of the "incorporation doctrine" is outside the scope of this article.

[139] 34 W. Blackstone, *Commentaries*, at 1326. While Blackstone is referring to the press specifically, I believe this quote is relevant to the overall discussion of freedom of speech without prior governmental restraint and responsibility of an individual for his speech and speech-related actions.

[140] 376 U.S. 254 (1964).

[141] *Id.* at 279–80.

[142] *Id.* Actual malice was defined by the Court as "knowledge that it was false or with reckless disregard of whether it was false or not." *Id.*

[143] *Id.* at 277. "'[T]he Constitution delimits a State's power' to award remedies for civil torts." *Braun v. Soldier of Fortune Magazine*, 968 F.2d 1110, 1116 (11th Cir. 1992) (citing *New York Times v. Sullivan*, 376 U.S. 254, 283 (1964)).

[144] *Id.* at 265.

[145] U.S. CONST. amend I.

[146] *Cohen v. California*, 403 U.S. 15 (1971).

[147] *Chaplinsky v. New Hampshire*, 315 U.S. 568 (1942).

[148] *Miller v. California*, 413 U.S. 15 (1973).

[149] Through the doctrine of "incorporation" making the First Amendment applicable to the States, and State laws through the Fourteenth Amendment, "Congress" in this context would include the legislative branch of both the State and Federal governments.

[150] *See* ROBERT O'NEIL, THE FIRST AMENDMENT AND CIVIL LIABILITY 20 (Indiana Univ. Press 2001).

[151] *Rosenblatt v. Baer*, 383 U.S. 75, 92 (1975).

[152] For an interesting approach to *Brandenburg*, see, David Crump, *Camouflaged Incitement: Freedom of Speech, Communicative Torts, and the Borderland of the Brandenburg Test*, 29 GA. L. REV. 1 (Fall 1994) ("But suits like [*] remind us that there is another side to *Brandenburg*. That case draws the line (or more accurately, suggests the general area where future cases may draw it), defining where speech ends and where unprotected utterances begin.").

[153] Brandenburg was convicted originally for " 'advocat(ing) *** the duty, necessity, or propriety of crime, sabotage, violence, or unlawful methods of terrorism as a means of accomplishing industrial or political reform' and for 'voluntarily assembl(ing) with any society, group, or assemblage of persons formed to teach or

advocate the doctrines of criminal syndicalism.' Ohio Rev. Code Ann. s [§] 2923.13."

[154] John Charles Kunich, *Natural Born Copycat Killers and the Law of Shock Torts*, 78 WASH. UNIV. L. Q. 1157, 1158 (2000).

[155] Referring to Judge Learned Hand's opinion, now legendary in both law and economics, in *United States v. Carroll Towing Co.*, 159 F.2d 169 (2d Cir. 1947), distilling liability into a mathematical, cost-benefit formula: "[p]ossibly it serves to bring this notion into relief to state it in algebraic terms: if the probability be called P; the injury, L; and the burden, B; liability depends upon whether B is less than L multiplied by P: i.e., whether B < PL."

[156] *Kunich*, at 1230.

[157] *See supra*, note 151 and accompanying text.

[158] *Kunich*, at 1230.

[159] *Id.* (emphasis added)

[160] It is interesting to note the general acceptance of the First Amendment in seemingly all situations where speech could potentially be "chilled" regardless of who might be doing the "chilling." Professor Kunich's article in explaining "[t]he applicable Frist Amendment principles in general" [heading] states: "[t]he primary legal impediment to recovery in media-related cases, quite naturally, has been the First Amendment…" The "quite naturally" language indicates the general acceptance of the place of the First Amendment in cases involving private parties. This article could be summed up generally as confronting the acceptance leading to the thought that the First Amendment would "quite naturally" create an impediment where one private party seeks legal relief in the form of money damages from another private parties in situations of "shock torts."

[161] For a historical perspective relevant to the content of *Hit Man*, *see*, *Frohwerk v. United States*: "We venture to believe that neither Hamilton nor Madison, nor any other competent person then or later, ever supposed that to make criminal the counselling [sic] of a murder within the jurisdiction of Congress would be an unconstitutional interference with free speech." *Frohwerk v. United States*, 249 U.S. 204, 206 (1919).

[162] *Rice*, 128 F.3d at 250.

[163] *Id.*

[164] *Id.* at 244.

[165] *Id.*

[166] *Kunich*, at 1158.

[167] Although the Fourth Circuit had held that *Brandenburg* was inapplicable for a different reason than my proposal that the First Amendment is not directly invoked in private tort suits.

[168] *Eimann v. Soldier of Fortune Magazine, Inc.*, 880 F.2d 830, 831 (5th Cir. 1989) (*Soldier of Fortune* magazine is a "publication that focuses on mercenary activities and military affairs.)

[169] *Eimann*, 880 F.2d at 831–32 ("Between early 1982 and January 1984, Black has asked at least four friends or coworkers from Bryan, Texas to kill Sandra Black or help him kill her. All four refused. Black called Hearn in October 1984 after seeing his ad in SOF.")

[170] A federal district court jury awarded Sandra Black's family $9.4 million. *SOF* appealed the verdict to the Fifth Circuit Court of Appeals. *Id.* at 831.

[171] *Id.* at 834.

[172] *Braun v. Soldier of Fortune Magazine, Inc.*, 986 F.2d 1110, 1112 (11th Cir. 1992).

[173] *Id.* at 1114.

[174] *Id.*

[175] Because it is not directly relevant in this section, I have excluded the 11th Circuit's handling of *SOF's* specific claims under the First Amendment. For extensive discussion, see *id*, at 1116.

[176] Note that *Norwood* is not part of this 'mini' circuit split and is a federal district court case, not a court of appeals decision.

[177] Michael I. Meyerson, *This Gun for Hire: Dancing in the Dark of the First Amendment*, 47 WASH. & LEE L. REV. 267, 276–77 (Winter 1990).

[178] *Norwood v. Soldier of Fortune, Inc.*, 651 F. Supp. 1397, 1400 (W.D. Ark. 1987).

[179] *Id.* at 1399–1400.

[180] 814 F.2d 1017 (5th Cir. 1987).

[181] *Id.* at 1018.

[182] *Id.*

[183] *Herceg v. Hustler Magazine, Inc.*, 814 F.2d 1017, 1025 (5th Cir. 1987) (Jones, Cir. Judge, dissenting). *See also Weirum v. RKO General, Inc.*, 123 Cal. Rptr. 468, 472 (1975).

Defendant's contention that the giveaway contest must be afforded the deference due society's interest in the First Amendment is clearly without merit. The issue here is civil accountability for the foreseeable results of a broadcast which created an undue risk of harm to decedent. The First Amendment does not sanction the infliction of physical injury merely because achieved by word, rather than act.

Id.

[184] *McCollum v. CBS Records*, 202 Cal. App. 3d 989, 1003 (1988).

[185] *Id.* at 1006.

[186] *Id.* at 1005–06.

[187] *Rice*, 128 F.3d at 239 n.1.

[188] *Id.* at 241. The court also noted that Perry had used a second Paladin Press book, *How to Make a Disposable Silencer, Vol. II*, to carry out the murders. *Id.*

[189] *Id.*

[190] *Id.*

[191] *Id.* at 266 (internal citation omitted).

[192] While most analysis of *Brandenburg* focuses on the "imminence" requirement, the thesis underlying this chapter in the book is that it is the "abstract" requirement of *Brandenburg* that is many times more relevant to the scope of the doctrine's protections. *See* Robert Firester and Kendall T. Jones, *Catchin' the Heat of the Beat: First Amendment Analysis of Music Claimed to Incite Violent Behavior*, 20 LOY. L.A. ENT. L. REV. 10 (2000) ("Most scholarly writing on the *Brandenburg* test has focused on the imminence requirement.")

[193] *Planned Parenthood v. Amer. Coalition of Life*, 290 F.3d 1058 1071 (9th Cir. 2002) (citations omitted). *See also Hess v. Indiana*, 414 U.S. 105 (1973); *NAACP v. Claiborne Hardware Co.*, 458 U.S. 886 (1982). *See also generally Rice v. Paladin Enterprises*, 128 F.3d 233, 243 (4th Cir. 1997).

[194] *Noto v. United States*, 367 U.S. 290, 297–98 (1961).

[195] *Brandenburg*, 395 U.S. at 449.

[196] 249 U.S. 47, 52 (1919).

[197] *Id.* at 446 n.1. The Court included "[the significant portions that could be understood…." *Id.*

[198] 414 U.S. 105 (1973).

[199] *Brandenburg v. Ohio*, 395 U.S. at 456 (Douglas, J., concurring).

[200] *Id.* (Douglas, J., concurring).

[201] *See* www.satanservice.org//coe/suicide/guide/#III (last visited Oct. 19, 2004). I hesitantly include this citation.

[202] The "Church's" "Four Pillars" are: suicide, abortion, cannibalism and sodomy. One of its mantras appears to be "Save the Planet—Kill Yourself."

[203] *Kunich*, at 1157.

[204] Grisham comments on the causal relationship between the movie and the murder of Bill Savage. Grisham asserts the question, "[w]ould Ben have shot innocent people but for the movie?" It should be remembered that if traditional tort analysis is utilized (as I have argued) in dealing with private parties such as Savage's estate and the *NBK* producers, etc., proximate causation (not the "but-for" test or factual causation) would still have to be established in order for the Plaintiff to properly recover damages. Grisham takes a different approach, focusing on a product liability cause of action.

[205] John Grisham, *Unnatural Killers*, OXFORD AMERICAN MAGAZINE, April 1996. (Reprinted with permission).

[206] 336 U.S. 77, 88 (1949).

[207] *Norwood v. Soldier of Fortune, Inc.*, 651 F. Supp. 1397, 1402 (W.D. Ark. 1987).

[208] 34 W. Blackstone, *Commentaries* at 1326. *See also* 16A Am.Jur.2d *Constitutional Law* § 506 at 343:

> Although freedom of speech or of the press under constitutional guarantees may not be altogether restrained, he who abuses the right may nevertheless be held to liability therefor. [sic] The First Amendment does not confer an absolute right to speak or publish, without responsibility, whatever one may choose. The extraordinary protections afforded by the First Amendment's guaranty of free speech and press carry with them something in the nature of a fiduciary duty to exercise the protected rights responsibly, a duty widely acknowledged but not always observed by editors and publishers. It does no violence to the value of freedom of speech and press to impose a duty of reasonable care upon those who would exercise such freedoms;

Id. (Ed. current as of 1987; used to illustrate historical perspective). *See also Norwood*, 651 F. Supp. at 1402–03.

[209] Everson v. Board of Ed. 330 U.S. 1, 16–18 (1947).

[210] Christopher Hitchens, *God and Man in the White House*, VANITY FAIR, Aug. 2003, at 76–81.

[211] The expansive scope of the Establishment clause was recently illustrated when the U.S. Supreme Court held that a Washington state statute that singled out and refused to fund devotional theology within the framework of a generally applicable scholarship program did not violate the First Amendment. *See Locke v. Davey*, 540 U.S. 712 (2004). Justice Scalia, in dissent, stated:

> That is precisely what the State of Washington has done here. It has created a generally available public benefit, whose receipt is conditioned only on academic performance, income, and attendance at an accredited school. It has then carved out a solitary course of study for exclusion: theology. Wash. Rev. Code § 28B.119.010(8) (Supp. 2004); Wash. Admin. Code § 250-80-020(12)(g) (2003). No field of study but religion is singled out for disfavor in this fashion. Davey is not asking for a special benefit to which others are not entitled. Cf. Lyng v. Northwest Indian Cemetery Protective Assn., 485 U.S. 439, 453, 108 S. Ct. 1319, 99 L. Ed. 2d 534 (1988). He seeks only equal treatment—the right to direct his scholarship to his chosen course of study, a right every other Promise Scholar enjoys.

Locke, 124 S. Ct. at 1316 (Scalia, J., dissenting). "One need not delve too far into modern culture to perceive a trendy disdain for deep religious conviction." *Id.* at 1320 (Scalia, J., dissenting). "What next? Will we deny priests and nuns their prescription-drug benefits on the ground that taxpayers' freedom of conscience forbids medicating the clergy at public expense?" *Id* at 1320 (Scalia, J., dissenting).

[212] The decision was handed down by the U.S. Supreme Court on June 14, 2004, which allowed for this brief footnote but did not allow for the ruling's full integration into the text of this book. On June 14, 2004, the U.S. Supreme Court reversed the ruling of the Ninth Circuit Court of Appeals, holding that "Newdow lack[ed] standing." *See Elk Grove Unified School District v. Newdow*, 542 U.S. ___ (2004). "There is a vast difference between Newdow's right to communicate with his child—which both California law and the First Amendment recognize—and his claimed right to shield his daughter from influences to which she is exposed in school despite the terms of the custody order. We conclude that, having been deprived under California law of the right to sue as next friend, Newdow lacks prudential standing to bring this suit in federal court." *Id.* at ___. One interesting note about the press coverage of the case, USA TODAY ran a headline proclaiming that the case was dismissed on a "technicality." I would not consider the "standing" requirement to file a suit in federal court to be a mere "technicality." *See generally Warth v. Seldin*, 422 U.S. 490, 498 (1975). Justice Scalia "took no part in the consideration or decision of [the *Elk Grove*] case."

[213] *See* Fox News, AP, *Justice Scalia to Stay Out of Pledge Case*, Oct. 15, 2003. "The remaining eight justices could deadlock 4-4. That would affirm the 9th U.S. Circuit Court of Appeal's ban on the religious reference, which would apply to 9.6 million schoolchildren in the nine states the court oversees: California, Oregon, Nevada, Montana, Washington, Idaho, Arizona, Hawaii and Alaska, plus Guam." *Id.*

214 *West Virginia State Board of Ed. v. Barnette*, 319 U.S. 624 (1943).

215 Just prior to this book going to print, the Ten Commandment controversy took on new momentum. On Tuesday, October 12, 2004 the U.S. Supreme Court announced that it would hear appeals involving the display of the Ten Commandments in Kentucky and Texas.

216 *Lambs Chapel v. Center Moriches Union Free School District*, 508 U.S. 384, 398 (1993) (Scalia, J., concurring). Interested readers should read Scalia's entire concurrence in *Lamb's Chapel*. It humorously and entertainingly pokes fun at, and holes in, the *Lemon*-test.

217 Referring to the "test" created by the U.S. Supreme Court in *Lemon v. Kurtzman*, 403 U.S. 602 (1971). I am using the original form of the test set forth in Lemon including the question of whether such state action fosters "an excessive government entanglement with religion." *Lemon*, 403 U.S. at 612–13. It is sometimes said that the U.S. Supreme Court folded this question into the "effect" prong of the overall inquiry. *See Agostini v. Felton*, 521 U.S. 203, 233 (1997).

218 *See* Marc M. Harrold, *Stripping Away at the First Amendment: The Increasingly Paternal Voice of our Living Constitution* 32 U. MEM. L. REV. 403, 408 (Winter 2002).

219 I have previously written an article related to the First Amendment and judicial elitism in the context of "adult entertainment." *See generally* Marc M. Harrold, *Stripping Away at the First Amendment: The Increasingly Paternal Voice of our Living Constitution*, 32 U. MEM. L. REV. 403 (Winter 2002). Here, I have used my original title, "*G-Strings, Pasties, Judicial Elitism and the Naked Truth of Crumbling Federalism*," because the editor at the University of Memphis Law Review suggested that I change the title of the article. He was right, of course, in suggesting the change.

220 Quote provided by noted First Amendment attorney Steve G. Mason, Esquire in an e-mail from Mason to author dated July 29, 2003. Mason practices in and around Orlando, Florida and has been involved in numerous high-profile First Amendment cases involving adult-entertainment.

221 *Salem Inn, Inc. v. Frank*, 501 F.2d 18, 21 n.3 (2d Cir. 1974), *aff'd in part, sub nom., Doran v. Salem Inn, Inc.*, 422 U.S. 922 (1975).

222 For further information on this exchange, *see*, Vincent Blasi, *Six Conservatives in Search of the First Amendment: the Revealing Case of Nude Dancing*, 33 WM. & MARY L. REV. 611 (1992) (noting in detailed discussion and opinions of Richard Posner, Frank Easterbrook, William Rehnquist, Antonin Scalia, David Souter, and Byron White with regards to the role of the First Amendment and nude dancing).

[223] *Miller v. City of South Bend*, 904 F.2d 1081 (7th Cir. 1990) (en banc).

[224] *Barnes v. Glen Theatre, Inc.* 501 U.S. 560 (1991).

[225] *Id.*

[226] *See PAP'S*, 529 U.S. at 310 (Scalia, J., concurring) ("Here, even if one hypothesizes that the city's object was to suppress only nude dancing, that would not establish an intent to suppress that (if anything) nude dancing communicates.").

[227] At least facially.

[228] 360 U.S. 684, 689 (1959) (citing *Whitney v. People of State of California*, 274 U.S. 357, 378 (1927)).

[229] *See, e.g.,* Reuters, *Klan Rally in Illinois Erupts in Violence,* CNN.com, (available at www.cnn.com/2000/US/12/16/klan.rally.reut./) (visited Aug. 7, 2003) (detailing violence between KKK members and anti-Klan demonstrators in the Chicago suburb of Skokie, Illinois.)

[230] 475 U.S. 41, 48 (1986).

[231] *Virginia v. Black*, 123 S. Ct. 1536, 1562 n. 2 (citing to *Renton*, 475 U.S. at 48) (emphasis added)

[232] 535 U.S. 234 (2002).

[233] *Id.*

[234] *Id.*

[235] *Id.*

[236] *Id.*

[237] *Id.* (emphasis added)

[238] *PAP's,* 529 U.S. at 317–18 (Stevens, J., dissenting) ("Until now, the "secondary effects" of commercial enterprises featuring indecent entertainment have justified only the regulation of their location. For the first time, the Court has now held that such effects may justify the total suppression of protected speech.") The expansion of the "secondary effects" doctrine to the point of an outright ban is also inconsistent with other U.S. Supreme Court opinions. *See, e.g., Ashcroft v. Free Speech Coalition,* 535 U.S. 234, 245 (2002) ("The prospect of crime, however, by itself does not justify law suppressing protected speech.") (additional citations omitted).

[239] *See, e.g., Renton v. Playtime Theatres, Inc.*, 475 U.S. 41 (1986).

[240] *See generally, PAP's,* 529 U.S. 277 (2000).

[241] Another disturbing development in the Court's use of "secondary effects" in relation to speech and speech conduct can be seen in the Court's 2002 ruling in *City of Los Angeles v. Alameda Books, Inc,* 535 U.S. 425 (2002).

[242] Even Scalia (who concurs in the opinion) is skeptical of the use of "secondary effects" in this context. *See PAP's*, 529 U.S. at 310 (Scalia, J., concurring) ("I do not feel the need, as the Court does, to identify some "secondary effects" associated with nude dancing that the city could properly seek to eliminate. (I am highly skeptical, to tell the truth, that the addition of pasties and G-strings will at all reduce the tendency of establishments such as Kandyland to attract crime and prostitution, and hence to foster sexually transmitted disease.").

[243] 337 F.3d 1251 (11th Cir. 2003).

[244] *Id.* at 1253.

[245] *Id.*

[246] *Id.*

[247] *Id.* at 1273–74.

[248] Assuming that it is a paid performance of *Hair*.

[249] As we have seen, the Supreme Court has not limited its determination of what is "essential" in the First Amendment context. Who can forget the Justices deciding what rules were or were not "essential" in the made up world of the game of golf?

[250] In an *amicus* brief filed in the *PAP's* case by Bill Conte, on behalf of the *Dante Project: Inferno* and the National Campaign for Freedom of Expression, in Support of PAP's, A.M., empirical evidence was offered to refute the Court's finding in *Barnes* that no significant deprivation of erotic message occurred when dancers are required to don G-strings and pasties:

> Psychologist Edward I. Donnerstein's study of exotic dance disproves the conclusion in Barnes v. Glen Theatre, Inc. that "the requirement that the dancers don pasties and a g-string does not deprive the dance of whatever erotic message it conveys; it simply makes the message slightly less graphic." [501 U.S. 560, 571 (1991)] The research demonstrates that nudity, as a component of exotic dance, is essential to the messages conveyed by such dance. Without it, the intended messages are substantially changed.

> ...

> The study reveals that men judge nude dancers to be communicating different messages than clothed dancers. Ultimately, the study concludes that a dancer donning pasties and a G-string conveys a significantly different message compared to when she is nude.

[251] Don't confuse this with the similarly titled section in PENTHOUSE magazine.

252 For more information about the case and Ron's struggle, check out the Freedom Tattoo website at www.freedomtattoo.com.

253 *State v. White*, 560 S.E.2d 420, 423 (S.C. 2002).

254 *Spence v. Washington*, 418 U.S. 405 (1974).

255 For fun, check out the www.ihatemimes.com website. I have nothing to do with this site, but it is worth a look.

256 *Bleistein v. Donaldson Lithographing Co.*, 188 U.S. 239, 252 (1903).

257 739 F. Supp. 578 (S.D. Fla. 1990).

258 *Id.* at 582.

259 *Id.* at 603. ("ORDERED AND ADJUDGED as follows: (1) The recording As Nasty As They Wanna Be created by the group 2 Live Crew is hereby DECLARED obscene....").

260 *Id.* at 586. (emphasis in original).

261 *Id.* (emphasis in original).

262 *Id.* at 582.

263 *Id.* at 587.

264 *Id.*

265 *Id.* at 586.

266 *Id.*

267 *Id.* at 587. (citation omitted).

268 *Id.* at 588.

269 *Id.* The Judge considers the following: (1) They are three adjoining counties that share common geography on the eastern coast of Florida; (2) They share space on the Atlantic Ocean and the resulting influx of tourists; (3) They are "open" communities that invite visitors who sometimes relocate to South Florida; (4) The three counties are linked by rail, water, air and highway; (5) The labor forces of the three counties commingle; (6) There is a sharing of media between the three media; (7) The three share cultural events; (8) The three counties are economically linked; (9) A similar composition of rural and urban areas; and (10) Political ties exist between the three counties. *Id.*

270 *Id.*

271 *Id.*

272 *Id.*

273 *Id.* (emphasis added).

274 *Id.*

275 *Id.*

276 *Id.* at 593.

277 *Id.*

278 *Id.* at 595.

279 *Id.* (citation omitted).

280 *Id.* at 596.

281 Originally the student was charged with disorderly conduct. This charge was later amended to the present charge.

282 In *Smith v. Mount Pleasant Public Schools,* 2003 WL 22290233 (E.D. Mich.), the District Court dealt with a somewhat similar set of facts. A student had been suspended under the school's "verbal assault" policy. The court held that the specific policy was both vague and overbroad but that the school, nonetheless, could discipline the student without violating the First Amendment. *Id.* at *. "The Court finds that the defendant's so-called "verbal assault" policy, and the enabling statute upon which it is based, are unconstitutionally vague and overbroad. However, the Court also finds that the defendant could properly discipline the plaintiff for his insulting remarks directed at school personnel, and that the discipline did not violate the plaintiff's First Amendment rights." *Id. See also In re Douglas D.,* 626 N.W.2d 725, 742 (Wisc. 2001) ("Although the First Amendment prohibits law enforcement officials from prosecuting protected speech, it does not necessarily follow that schools may not discipline students for such speech.").

283 Two parts of this paragraph appear to me to be problematic. First, it is only a crime to yell "Fire" if you are doing so "falsely"; if there is actually a "fire" it is OK to yell "Fire," although there may be a more prudent way to go about warning people. Second, if you yell "Fuck!" in a theatre you are likely going to be asked to leave and if you don't, charged with disturbing the peace or disorderly conduct. The brief seems to indicate that there isn't any way to criminalize yelling "Fuck!" in a theatre. I think that this reading, in an attempt to make the valid distinction, is too broad.

284 I started these observations by charging readers that we must continue to strive to discover and fully understand both the optimal need and "core meaning" of the First Amendment. In closing, the remedy to any of the expression-related challenges facing our rapidly advancing technologically-based, information driven culture is not found in the restriction of speech, but in the enlargement of it. Our "marketplace of ideas," can and should be similarly viewed as a "marketplace economy of ideas" where, mirroring other lessons of a market-driven economy, we find that all societal solutions do not require or invite judicial action or resolve, or even governmental involvement generally. "Under our Constitution 'there is no such thing as a false idea. However pernicious an opinion may seem, we depend for its correction not on the conscience of judges and juries but on the

competition of other ideas.' Gertz v. Robert Welsh, Inc., 418 U.S., at 339–340, 94 S. Ct., at 3007 (footnote omitted)."

978-0-595-37248-5
0-595-37248-1